THE AFRICAN AMERICAN CHRISTIAN NATION!

THE HEALING BALM
FOR A DISTINCT PEOPLE

by **Mark C. Olds**

THE
AFRICAN
AMERICAN
CHRISTIAN
NATION

MARK C. OLDS

"The disenfranchisement of the African American people must cease. The people with the mind of Christ must unite and seize the opportunity for nationhood!...The same as the Jewish nation, the African American Christian Nation simply wishes to exercise the right to be obedient to all that God has given as instructions to follow in governing ourselves."

The Reverend Mark C. Olds

Community Resource Inc.
3550 Warrensville Center Road
Suite 101, South
Shaker Heights, Ohio 44122
(216) 752-5559

ISBN 0-9648423-0-0

Acknowledgements

A very special thanks to my wife, Linda, for her unwavering support and commitment. Thanks to Sister Wife for the love and consistency of encouragement while working to complete her graduate studies!

Thank you to Rev. Dr. Margaret Mitchell and Brother Gary Morton for their covenant friendship and straightforward insight in editing this work. I appreciate the time given to this project away from their marriage and extremely busy schedules.

Thank you to Barbara Campbell and Edith Barnes, friends from my childhood, who understand tangible help along with prayers.

Published By:

COMMUNITY RESOURCE INC.
3550 WARRENSVILLE CENTER ROAD
SUITE 101, SOUTH
SHAKER HEIGHTS, OHIO 44122
(216) 752-5559

Dedication

To my late parents,

**Willie Grey Olds and
Ida Mae Olds**

Contents

SECTION ONE

Why the Struggle to Be a Nation?

SECTION TWO

What Is the Pillar for the Nation?

SECTION THREE

How to Enact the Nation?

Preface

" In these difficult times, and this era of repression, I believe God has given me a clear message to take to the people of color living in these United States. This is a clear message to the more than thirty million people of color living in this country. It is a message of salvation, deliverance, healing, and economic stability and progress. It is a message to birth a nation, 'The African American Christian Nation.'"[1]

Pastor Mark C. Olds
African Americans:
A Nation Unborn Crusade, 1994

The emergence of the African American Christian Nation is an awakening to people trapped in religiosity to the fact that God still works. He is concerned (hands on) with the evolution and progress of His man. God has not completed all that He is

---

[1]Olds, Pastor Mark C., *African Americans: A Nation Unborn Crusade.* An excerpt from a sermon preached in Greenville, North Carolina, 1994.

going to perform. He is not now reclining unattentatively to man's activities waiting to see how the affairs of the world play out. As new challenges appear, God is in the midst of warfare. He teaches our hands to war. His instructions are key to victories over the most brilliant designs of bondage.

"The grounding of liberation in God's act in Jesus Christ is the logical consequence of any Christian theology that takes Scripture seriously as an important source for the doing theology....Black people can fight for freedom and justice, because the One who is their future is also the ground of their struggle for liberation."[2]

James H. Cone
God of the Oppressed

Oppressed people win, because God is a God of liberation. God pours Himself by His Spirit into yielded vessels who are raised from weakness to strength. Freedom is a gift from God. No man is able to take away the freedom of the spirit extended to those who abide in the Lord. God judges and destroys those who oppose His plans.

This work is not a cry for Christians to launch a new church congregation or a denomination. Its intent is to raise the consciousness of African Americans to the level of becoming a nation. This work

---

[2]Cones, James H., *God of the Oppressed.* New York: The Seabury Press, Inc., 1975, pgs. 139-140.

will explore the steps necessary to become a nation or lay the foundational steps for becoming a nation. Upon reaching the level of nationhood thinking, it is then easy to grasp the initiative to progress toward being a nation. This is not some grandiose idea to make oppressed people feel good with a momentary spiritual and intellectual mix of theoretical impossibility. The content of this work involves both the resolution and the determination to propel African Americans to occupy the position where God has called them, to nationhood. The African American Christian Nation is a great evangelistic tool. It is an outreach to those who have not yet embraced the Gospel of Jesus Christ.

The divine activity in African American people has not diminished throughout years of oppression. This divine activity is ready to unfold the birth of a new nation. No matter what the level of aggression by the oppressor, divine assertion is able to give birth to the supernatural. The dominant forces are always unprepared for the unseen. God's people have to be the opposite. Saints must learn to always rely on the promises of God. *"For I will drive out nations before you and enlarge your borders."* (Exodus 34:24, NASB)

The end results of this work is to provide people of African descent (residing in America) a faith walk to the place God has designed for them. When the course enacted by the ruling powers conflict with God's arranging of things, He is still able to deliver the people who suffer injustice. God is still very active in affairs of the African American people. He is able to bring down those who oppose the steps of a people ordered to nationhood by God.

> *"Thine, O Lord, is the greatness and the power and the glory and the victory and the majesty, indeed everything that is in the heavens and the earth; Thine is the dominion, O Lord, and Thou dost exalt Thyself as head over all. Both riches and honor come from Thee, and Thou dost rule over all, and in Thy hand is power and might; and it lies in Thy hand to make great, and to strengthen everyone."*
> (1 Chronicles 29:11,12, NASB)

The power to raise up the African American Christian Nation is within God's sovereignty. The birth of this nation does not depend upon whether or not any group of human minds think it is a good idea or not!

God is not bound by what is visible to manifest a new nation. Eras and ages cannot lock the Almighty out of the birthing of a new nation. The salvation of a people is of greater importance than the maintenance of existing conditions which repress potential. God's intervention into the affairs of the nations of the world to produce a new nation that will obey Him and administer justice demonstrates His perfect timing in all things. God is still the Lord of creation. He is still able to speak that which is not into being. He knows when existing systems and orders must be shown a new standard of moral excellence and consecrated holiness.

"Let the name of God be blessed forever and ever, For wisdom and power belong to Him. And it is He who changes the times and the epochs; He removes kings and establishes kings; He gives wisdom to wise men, And knowledge to men of understanding. It is He who reveals the profound and hidden things; He knows what is in the darkness, And the light dwells with Him." (Daniel 2:20-22, NASB)

This work is designed to bring to light the next step in the long struggle for freedom by African American people. The absence of a vehicle to carry African Americans to their rightful place is not a justifiable excuse anymore. This work will introduce the African American Christian Nation as the vehicle with the power to reach the destination of nationhood. There is no longer the great battlefield of debate of what can or cannot be done. The endless rounds of dialogue of why we cannot come together as a people are no longer valid. It is the firm declaration of this author that nationhood for African American people will eradicate mysteries surrounding their alienation from global policy making, myths of inferiority will be eliminated, and the fear of failure as a people eradicated! This work will demonstrate that nationhood for African American people is a sovereign move of the Holy Spirit!

"Declaring the end from the beginning, And from ancient times things which have not been done, Saying, 'My purpose will be established, And I will accomplish all My good pleasure'; Calling a bird of prey from the east, The man of My purpose from a far country. Truly I have spoken; truly I will bring it to pass. I have planned it, surely I will do it....The smallest one will become a clan, And the least one a mighty nation. I, the Lord, will hasten it in its time....Encourage the exhausted, and strengthen the feeble. Say to those with palpitating heart, Take courage, fear not. Behold, your God will come with vengeance; The recompense of God will come, But He will save you.' Then the eyes of the blind will be opened, And the ears of the deaf will be unstopped. Then the lame will leap like a deer, And the tongue of the dumb will shout for joy....And a highway will be there, a roadway, And it will be called 'the highway of holiness.' The unclean will not travel on it, But it will be for him who walks that way, And fools will not wander on it." (Isaiah 46:10,11; 60:22 and 35:3-6,8, NASB)

Introduction

The body of people which has emerged into African Americans was never intended to be a part of the colonized "New World." It was not until it was discovered that Africans could be brutalized into a cheap labor pool (slavery) that they were considered for occupancy on the shores of the "New World."

"Although Africans were in Europe in considerable numbers in the seventeenth century and had been in the New World at least since 1501, the European imperalist did not at first regard them as a solution to their labor problems. To be sure, Africans were being employed, but the colonist and their Old World sponsors were extremely slow in recognizing them as the best possible labor force for the tasks in the New World. Before they came to see this, they resorted to the poor whites of Europe. In the first half of the seventeenth century, they brought these landless, penniless whites over to do the work of clean-

ing the forests and cultivating the fields. When the supply of those who voluntarily indentured themselves for a period of years proved insufficient, the English resorted to more desperate means. Their desperation is clearly seen in the emergence of the widespread practice of kidnapping children, women, prisoners, and drunken men....England came to realize that white servants were unsatisfactory....Englishmen began to ask themselves why they should be concerned with white servants when blacks presented so few of the difficulties encountered with the whites. Because of their color, Negroes could easily be apprehended. Furthermore, they could be purchased outright and a master's labor supply would not be in a state of constant fluctuation. Negroes, from a pagan land and without exposure to the ethical ideals of Christianity, could be handled with more rigid methods of discipline and could be morally and spiritually degraded for the sake of stability on the plantation. In the long run, Negro slaves were actually cheaper. In a period when economic considerations were so vital, this was especially important. Negro slavery, then, became a fixed institution, a solution to one of the most difficult New World problems. With the supply of Africans apparently inexhaustible, there would be no more worries about labor."[3]

John Hope Franklin
From Slavery to Freedom

---

[3]Franklin, John Hope. *From Slavery to Freedom,* New York: Alfred A. Knopf, Inc., 1988, pgs. 31-32.

It is important to note that Africans did not come to this country as immigrants. That may be difficult for some to believe, but it is true. Africans were the only people brought to the Western Hemisphere against their will. Coming to America was not a voluntary immigration pattern by Africans.

During the colonization of the "New World" to further substantiate the European claim to the exclusion of Africans from partaking in the "New World"; Africans were not considered human and therefore could not hope for citizenship. This exclusion of Africans from equal status by the founding fathers of the United States of America is a tremendous blessing for African Americans. This means that African Americans will not have to answer to God for the brutality and thievery of the lands and resources of the Native Americans! God has again revealed Himself as the God of the oppressed!

"In 1790, Congress passed the first naturalization law, decreeing that America would open its doors to 'white immigrants only.' In 1994, out of 700,000 legal immigrants admitted, under 3% were African, some of them white."[4]

Barbara Reynolds,
Columnist, *USA Today*

---

[4]Reynolds, Barbara, columnist. *USA Today,* Gannet Company, 1995.

The realization is that a people has emerged to over thirty million in strength who were never meant to be a part of this "New World." Struggles for equal rights have been great and should not be overlooked or discounted. The larger issue is that God's plan has brought this people to a place where they might achieve His purpose. Equal status with others before God would simply mean being a nation the same as others.

Of course, there is a "New World Order" on the horizon. The same as that other "New World," African Americans have been purposely excluded by the founding fathers of this "New World Order." It is imperative that the African American Christian Nation arise at such a time as this. It is time for African Americans to become "founding fathers" of the path which leads to its divine destiny!

This is possible when the six necessary components which distinguishes a nation are viewed from God's Word. First, nation has to be defined. Webster puts forth the following definition: *nation —a stable, historically developed of people with a territory, economic life, distinctive culture, and language in common.* Each of these points contained in the definition must be explored.

STABLE:

To be considered stable, a people have to be firmly established. To be recognized by others as a nation, a people have to be firmly established in who they are as a people! The ambivalent inward emotional struggle regarding American patriotism is a perspective many African Americans have to settle in order to gain a sober reality of their identity. The emotional demand is stablized when African Americans have a clear understanding of their involvement and participation in the existing system of power. A great enlightenment arises when it is clearly differentiated between being a part of a system without any choice as opposed to gaining an option of full participation in a system by choice! This exercise of choice enables a people to hold steady to their faith in God while the oppression of men swells! What is acceptable and pleasing to men can rise to be a stink in the nostrils of God.

The question of whether or not African Americans should abandon America need not arise. That is not the issue at all. The issue is the mandate from God to be a nation. When the path to nationhood is chosen, a great stability emerges to walk in the destiny preordained by God for all people which is to be a nation. The demonstration of patriotic fervor has nothing to do with carrying out the plan and purpose of God! *"Righteousness exalteth a nation: but sin is a reproach to any people." (Proverbs 14:34, KJV)* It is righteousness which will exalt African American people from a life of reproach, not patriotic fervor or conservative ideology.

The birth of African descendants into a system that did not want them and only used them as profitable chattel has not provided a welcomed road to acceptance. The road has led through desegregation of physical facilities, but never allowing for creative integration. This fine line has kept alive the atmosphere for the emergence of the African American Christian Nation. This human birthing into a chattel system has left an environment where being stable is next to impossible. Thanks be to God that what is impossible with men is possible with God. Being stable means to be mentally healthy and well balanced. A people who have survived slavery, Jim Crow (No Way), separate but equal, and a new contract with America which again does not include them, can only open their eyes to see that God is truly leading them. Without God there is no way this people could lay claim to any form of stability and be consistently well balanced and mentally healthy.

When the lack of opportunity on multiple fronts and the aggregation of dislike by the dominant society have seemingly taken their toll, African Americans have been able to successfully retain stability by calling on God. In the midst of the greatest turmoil and satanic schemes of destruction, this people have found an anchor for the rising nation.

"The Lord is exalted, for He dwells on high; He has filled Zion with justice and righteousness. And He shall be the stability of your times, A wealth of salvation, wisdom, and knowledge; The fear of the Lord is his treasure." (Isaiah 33:5,6, NASB)

When all else fails, God is able to be the stability of the African American Christian Nation. With faith in Him through Jesus Christ, steps are not taken in fear of what men may say, do, or how they may choose to react. The fear is in the Lord. He alone orders the steps of righteous men and women. As pressures mount and they surely will on the journey of such a vast undertaking as nationhood, it is most important that the first step taken is being born again by the Spirit. With this first step as the blessed assurance of stability, the channel of communication remains open. This open channel allows a people on the nationhood trail to be able to utter in difficulties, *"Like a swallow, like a crane, so I twitter; I moan like a dove;...O Lord, I am oppressed, be my security."* *(Isaiah 38:14, NASB)*

God's hearing and answering of the corporate prayer of people enlists them to stay steady in purpose. Over the years, the focus of the leadership and the people have vacillated. However, the Divine Destiny of God makes steady the helm and a clear vision emerges before the people. Each reemergence of stability within the people is more encompassing than the preceding episode of the walk by faith. African Americans more than any other group, have had to constantly prove resilience despite the many exploitations and diversions. This people has proven to be durable and endurable. These people are continually having to overcome external influences which have caused internal conflict. To stand today and speak of nationhood for African Americans is proof of this group's ability to be resistant to chemical and physical change. Legal and illegal chemical industries have not been able to destroy this people. The image campaign to alter physical appearance, because of a propagandizing to hate oneself has not been able to destroy this people.

This people is a group which is lasting. Longevity alone will not necessarily attest to the stability of this people, but longevity consummated with faith in God established the stability of the African Americans. A key component of being a nation is stability. African Americans have far exceeded definitions which can be contrived to mean stability.

HISTORICALLY DEVELOPED OF PEOPLE:

In order to be a nation the African American Christian Nation must be able to extend itself beyond its biological heritage. African Americans have a rich heritage which goes far across the waters of the Atlantic. This people did not commence its development on the shores of America. Their history goes far beyond a brutal system of slavery and oppression. Oppression is a kind term in relation to the inhumane acts of slavery in the western world.

"The slave trade left a bloodstained legacy. During the four centuries the trade was pursued, it wrecked the social and economic life of Africa, set nation against nation and village against village. The

trade was no less disastrous in Europe and America where it left a legacy of ill will and guilt and a potentially explosive racial problem.

"'Raphael painted,' W.E.B. DuBois said, 'Luther preached, Corneille wrote, and Milton sang; and through it all, for four hundred years, the dark captives wound to the sea amid the bleaching bones of the dead; for four hundred years the sharks followed the scurrying ships; for four hundred years America was strewn with the living and dying millions of a transplanted race; for four hundred years Ethiopia stretched forth her hands unto God.'"[5]

Lerone Bennett, Jr.
Before the Mayflower
Fifth Edition, Johnson
Publishing Company, Inc., 1982

The African American Christian Nation must rely on the Word of God in all phases of its existence. God's account of the people of African descent is a rich resource. God has never lost sight of this people or their seed. The grace of God is so amazing that wherever the seed of those of African descent has landed, He is able to raise up a nation.

The Prophet Jeremiah wrote of God's commitment to people of African descent. The Rechabites were of the Kenites, a Midianite tribe who came to Canaan from Africa with the Israelites. The sons of

---

[5]Bennett, Jr. Lerone. *Before the Mayflower.* Chicago: Johnson Publishing Company, 1976, pg. 54.

Rechab, the Rechabites, were faithful in their obedience to not pollute themselves with the gods of Palestine although Israel forsook the Lord.

> *"And the children of the Kenite, Moses' father in law, went up out of the city of palm trees with the children of Judah into the wilderness of Judah, which lieth in the south of Arad; and they went and dwelt among the people."* (Judges 1:16, KJV)
>
> *"And the families of the scribes which dwelt at Jabez; the Tirathites, the Shimeathites, and Suchathites. These are the Kenites that came of Hemath, the father of the house of Rechab."* (1 Chronicles 2:55, KJV)

The significance of Jeremiah's writing of this people is God's covenant with them.

> *"The words of Jonadab the son of Rechab, which he commanded his sons not to drink wine, are observed. So they do not drink wine to this day, for they have obeyed their father's command. But I have spoken to you again and again; yet you have not listened to Me. Also I have sent to you all My servants the prophets, sending them again and again, saying, 'Turn now every man from his evil way, and amend your deeds, and do not go after*

other gods to worship them, then you shall dwell in the land which I have given to you and to your forefathers; but you have not inclined your ear or listened to Me. Indeed, the sons of Jonadab the son of Rechab have observed the command of their father which he commanded them, but this people has not listened to Me.' Therefore thus says the Lord, the God of hosts, the God of Israel, 'Behold, I am bringing on Judah and on all the inhabitants of Jerusalem all the disaster that I have pronounced against them; because I spoke to them but they did not listen, and I have called them but they did not answer.' Then Jeremiah said to the house of the Rechabites, 'Thus says the Lord of hosts, the God of Israel, Because you have obeyed the command of Jonadab your father, kept all his commands, and done according to all that he commanded you; therefore thus says the Lord of hosts, the God of Israel, Jonadab the son of Rechab shall not lack a man to stand before Me always.'"
(Jeremiah 35:14-19, NASB)

God's covenant with the people of African descent cannot be broken. Wherever there are people of African descent willing to obey God, He will champion their cause and pour out His blessings upon them.

African Americans suffered the lost of their genealogy through the "making of a slave" process. The foremost steps to produce a successful slave was to destroy family, language, culture or customs, and religious practice. Having been raped in all these areas, African Americans cannot claim a physical birthright with the Rechabites or any other nation on the continent of Africa. However, the higher law of God states that wherever people obey Him, there will exist a sovereign move of God. The Lord of hosts is a God who does not change. He moves to act in covenant with all who pursue righteousness.

> *"For when Gentiles who do not have the Law do instinctively the things of the Law, these, not having the Law, are a law to themselves, in that they show the work of the Law written in their hearts, their conscience bearing witness, and their thoughts alternately accusing or else defending them, on the day when, according to my gospel, God will judge the secrets of men through Christ Jesus."* (Romans 2:14-16, NASB)

The destruction of the slaves in America's family history makes the genealogy connection with a specific people in Africa impossible to trace or document. Therefore the reliance on God's Word for the African American Christian Nation is more imperative than a mere religious option. Yet, God still pursues a covenant relationship with African Americans. *"The secret of the Lord is for those who fear Him, And He will make them know His covenant." (Psalm 25:14, NASB)* The good news for the African American Christian Nation is the continual revelations by God of Himself to a people who seek Him!

The Apostle Paul wrote with great emphasis on God's revealing His covenant relationship to all who obey His commands.

> *"For he is not a Jew who is one outwardly; neither is circumcision that which is outward in the flesh. But he is a Jew who is one inwardly; and circumcision is that which is of the heart, by the Spirit, not by the letter; and his praise is not from men."* (Romans 2:28,29, NASB)

Obedience is the key to the realization of the African American Christian Nation.

An Ethiopian eunuch was reading the book of Isaiah, when the Evangelist Philip was directed to him by the Holy Spirit. This Ethiopian was already a worshipper of God for he was returning from worshipping at Jerusalem. The Ethiopian eunuch, a court official, was in charge of the treasure of the Candace, queen of Ethiopia.

> *"And the eunuch answered Philip and said, 'Please tell me, of whom does the prophet say*

this? Of himself, or of someone else?' And Philip opened his mouth, and beginning from this Scripture he preached Jesus to him. And as they went along the road they came to some water; and the eunuch said, 'Look! Water! What prevents me from being baptized?' And Philip said, 'If you believe with all your heart, you may.' And he answered and said, 'I believe that Jesus Christ is the Son of God.' And he ordered the chariot to stop; and they both went down into the water, Philip as well as the eunuch; and he baptized him. And when they came up out of the water, the Spirit of the Lord snatched Philip away; and the eunuch saw him no more, but went on his way rejoicing." (Acts 8:34-39, NASB)

God remains faithful to the people of African descent. Slaves in America heard the Gospel and responded as did the Ethiopian court official of the Queen of Ethiopia. The slaves were people of noble descent. While they were enslaved in America, they called upon the same God that Jeremiah wrote of who had made a covenant promise to the Rechabites.

The African American Christian Nation will emerge historically developed of the people. It has deep spiritual development as demonstrated from the Scriptures. It also has noble historical development as descendants of the mighty nations which were the cultural and intellectual centers of the world.

The African Americans are a people who have a great claim to the events of history. Their destiny of becoming a nation is verified by the Word of God. The promise to the Rechabites is the same as the promise made to David the king. God kept His promise to David and God will keep His promise to the descendants of Rechab. God will also keep His promise to live in covenant with the African descendants now known as African Americans. Their place as a nation will surely arise in splendor by the grace of God!

TERRITORY:

A territory is a region or district. Men have assigned other men geographical territories, because of conquest or power. When other men exercise the authority to assign territories to other people, these territories are usual viewed as inferior. This inferior connotation plants the suggestion of undesirable; thereby, the inhabitants of the assigned territory never really accept ownership. In America, the people who have inhabited these assigned territories have mostly been assigned underclass status (socially and financially). These territories which the underclass have been assigned have borne the names reservations, slums, ghettos, or inner cities. The association of these terms with land mass has symbolized nonownership. Since nonownership is the mental projection and since little economic value has resulted in no desire to own the territory, the establishment of a nation has not been a practical pursuit. This has been due mostly in part to the notion that ownership of territory is the prerequisite to being a nation. This would be true, except that the territory is simply the place where a nation is positioned for a specific moment. A territory is basically the region or district of the base of operation for a nation. The nation of Israel was very much a nation as the two million plus people wandered (because of disobedience to God) in the desert for forty years. The nation of Israel's arrival into Canaan territory did not make them a nation. They were already a nation. In fact, they were already called the nation of Israel while slaves in the land of Goshen.

African American people do not have to have land to form an African American Christian Nation. The African American Christian Nation is not dependent upon the ownership of a land mass to be a nation. It can exist in the physical territory where the people are abiding. God alone sets the boundaries of a nation.

> *"And hath made of one blood all nations of men for to dwell on all the face of the earth, and hath determined the times before appointed, and the bounds of their habitation."*
> (Acts 17:26, KJV)

The people do not have to concern themselves about the land mass but rather about their continuous obedience to God.

The struggle in this country to perpetuate an existing system does not in anyway prohibit the people who are moving in faith and trusting God. *"The earth is the Lord's, and all it contains, The world, and those who dwell in it."* (Psalm 24:1, NASB) The elements necessary for a territory will be provided by the owner of the earth. African Americans have a provision of territory granted by God. He is responsible to make the provision at the proper season. He has promised a safe and peaceful habitation. *"Then my people will live in a peaceful habitation, And in secure dwellings and in undisturbed resting places."* (Isaiah 32:18, NASB) This promise from God assures that no outside influences can deny what He chooses to bring to fruition. In the midst of hostility and opposition God is still able to provide divine protection. *"When a man's ways are pleasing to the Lord, He makes even his enemies to be at peace with him."* (Proverbs 16:7, NASB)

ECONOMIC LIFE:

A basic component for being a nation is an economic life. The satisfaction of the material needs of a people is the economic life of the people. No one can doubt the presence of an economic life among African Americans. African Americans have an economic life which is counted on by many. In fact, African Americans have become the target of trendsetting, exploitative marketing campaigns.

Nationhood is not built on the control of resources. The myth is that a nation's strength rests in its ability to control resources. This myth causes one to conclude that people without resources are people without a nation. This train of thought works only for the dominant culture and those who have bought into the dominant culture's philosophy.

Obedience to God is the foundation of a nation having an economic life. The Israelites were a slave people without a land mass or control of resources. However, God gave them a plan by which they were able to leave Egypt a wealthy people. God is able to provide for a nation an economic life which will satisfy the material needs of the people.

> *"And I will shake all nations, and the desire of all nations shall come: and I will fill this house with glory, saith the LORD of hosts. The silver is mine, and the gold is mine, saith the LORD of hosts."* (Haggai 2:7,8, KJV)
>
> *"The earth is the Lord's, and all it contains, The world, and those who dwell in it."* (Psalm 24:1, NASB)

Provisions have never been short with God.

> *"For every beast of the forest is Mine, The cattle on a thousand hills. I know every bird of the mountains, And everything that moves in the field is Mine."* (Psalm 50:10,11, NASB)

The Lord requires obedience from any nation and He in turn will supply the economic life. As provider, God wants to be established as the economic life of a nation. An obedient nation does not have to rely on the frenzy of economic projections from the minds of men.

> *"Now it shall be, if you will diligently obey the Lord your God, being careful to do all His commandments which I command you today, the Lord your God will set you high above all the nations of the earth. And all these blessings shall come upon you and overtake you, if you will obey the Lord your God."* (Deuteronomy 28:1,2, NASB)

The Prophet Micah makes it plain what those commandments are.

> *"He has told you, O man, what is good; And what does the Lord require of you But to do justice, to love kindness, And to walk humbly with your God?"* (Micah 6:8, NASB)

The conditions which currently plague the majority of the African American people can be altered by obedience to God. The humbling of the spirit presents the opportunity for divine intervention.

> *"If I shut up heaven that there be no rain, or if I command the locusts to devour the land,*

or if I send pestilence among the people; If my people, which are called by my name, shall humble themselves, and pray, and seek my face, and turn from their wicked ways; then will I hear from heaven, and will forgive their sin, and will heal their land." (2 Chronicles 7:13,14, KJV)

The emergence of the African American Christian Nation would merely be another occasion for the miraculous power of God to bear witness that He is alive and works in the affairs of men and nations.

DISTINCTIVE CULTURE:

Every nation has a distinctive culture and African Americans are no exception. In the unfolding of a people, there are always the markings which clearly relate to their particular form of societal practices. These practices of culture will be the distinctive mark of identification of belonging to a particular people. It can become perilous not to retain one's cultural practices. Without the loyalty to retain distinctive culture expressions, acculturation easily takes place. This process results in the absorption of distinguishable patterns and practices of another people. Identity is then lost or abandoned.

In order to control a people, the dominant system most often relied on the stripping of the oppressed culture.

"To compare the words, the overt consciousness, of gospel songs with their style and performance is to reveal what appears to be a conundrum. While the message of black gospel music manifested the dissolution of the traditional sacred world and a high degree of acculturation to a modern religious consciousness, its style and performance were being revitalized by an intensified connection with the roots of traditional Afro-American religion and the sounds and styles of the twentieth-century secular music of the black community. This apparent paradox can serve as a model for the type of acculturation that has characterized black America in the twentieth century. Negro acculturation has often taken place within and been facilitated by a communal milieu. It has not been a simple one-dimensional process of switching allegiances or identities or life-styles. It has been a complex process of shifting emphases and reaffirmations: of permitting certain new traits to permeate but of simultaneously reemphasizing specific traditional loyalties and characteristics."[6]

Lawrence W. Levine
Black Culture and Black Consciousness

African slaves (which included those of royal seed and nobles among their people), coming from West Africa to the eastern shores of America were stripped of their linguistic, cultural, and religious freedom.

---

[6]Levine, Lawrence W., *Black Culture and Black Consciousness*. New York: Oxford University Press, 1978, pg. 189.

They were given a new role in a society that made the rules to keep them in permanent underclass status. This was not a new tactic. Daniel and his friends underwent the same subjection.

> *"Then the king ordered Ashpenaz, the chief of his officials, to bring in some of the sons of Israel, including some of the royal family and of the nobles, youths in whom was no defect, who were good looking, showing intelligence in every branch of wisdom, endowed with understanding, and discerning knowledge, and who had ability for serving in the king's court; and he ordered him to teach them the literature and language of the Chaldeans. And the king appointed for them a daily ration from the king's choice food and from the wine which he drank, and appointed that they should be educated three years, at the end of which they were to enter the king's personal service. Now among them from the sons of Judah were Daniel, Hananiah, Mishael and Azariah. Then the commander of the officials assigned new names to them; and to Daniel he assigned the name Belteshazzar, to Hananiah Shadrach, to Mishael Meshach, and Azariah Abed-nego."*
> (Daniel 1:3-7, NASB)

This is an example of manipulation into a new societal norm. The exchange of culture and affiliation.

The king ordered a distinct pattern to cause these young men to lose their identity and take the identity (names) assigned them from another distinct culture.

The key factor in ancient countries when defeating another nation was to destroy their place(s) of worship or capture their most sacred symbol of the deity they worshipped. The conquering army would make the proclamation that the defeated nation's god was not able to help or deliver them. As part of the surrender conditions of Japan to the United States at the end of World War II, the emperor of Japan had to renounce that he was deity. When a people cannot receive aid from their god, they are totally controllable.

Sennacherib, king of Assyria, invaded Judah during the reign of Hezekiah. He sent his messenger to proclaim in the hearing of all the people of Judah.

> *"Beware lest Hezekiah misleads you, saying, 'The Lord will deiiver us.' Has anyone of the gods of the nations delivered his land from the hand of the king of Assyria? Where are the gods of Hamath and Arpad? Where are the gods of Sepharvaim? And when have they delivered Samaria from my hand? Who among all the gods of these lands have delivered their land from my hand, that the Lord should deliver Jerusalem from my hand?'"* (Isaiah 36:18-20, NASB)

God is not intimidated by the powers that are in existence. The armies of men are of no major concern to God. He is all powerful. God's victory ability is not dependent upon the number of men enlisted in a physical army. *"Then the angel of the Lord went out, and struck 185,000 in the camp of the Assyrians; and when men arose early in the morning, behold, all of these were dead."* (Isaiah 37:36, NASB) African Americans have the Lord of hosts to call upon. He is the Almighty God who has never lost a battle. The Africans survived because they shifted their loyalty to the God of Moses. They saw themselves as the children of Israel. This gave them sustaining hope.

The opposition of a nation will attempt great measures to destroy a distinctive culture. The dissolvement of a nation's distinctive culture also dissolves the nation's faith in God. A nation without faith in God can easily be destroyed or possessed.

LANGUAGE IN COMMON:

There must be a mutual means of communication among a people to be a nation. This communication is reflected in the extended acts of cultural practice. It is also paramount for a people working toward common goals and retaining camaraderie to support one another.

> *"Youths in whom was no defect, who were good looking, showing intelligence in every*

branch of wisdom, endowed with understanding, and discerning knowledge, and who had ability for serving in the king's court; and he ordered him to teach them the literature and language of the Chaldeans." (Daniel 1:4, NASB)

The support mechanism is broken, when a nation is not speaking the same language on issues. The unity of a nation is dissolved when a new language and culture is introduced to the people.

The African slaves were not allowed to be placed together if they came from the same region and spoke the same language. This was deliberately done to break any support or possible insurrections. The slaves in Haiti were able to carry out a successful revolt, because the command to launch the attack was conveyed by drums.

God recognizes the importance of a nation speaking the same language. *"And the Lord said, 'Behold, they are one people, and they all have the same language. And this is what they began to do, and now nothing which they purpose to do will be impossible for them."* (Genesis 11:6, NASB) The foundation for success as a nation is to be a people speaking the same language and obeying the Word of God. A nation that has a single language to praise and worship God will discover that nothing which they purpose will be too hard for them to accomplish!

SECTION ONE

Why the Struggle to Be a Nation?

"For if thou altogether holdest thy peace at this time, then shall there enlargement and deliverance arise to the Jews from another place; but thou and thy father's house shall be destroyed: and who knoweth whether thou art come to the kingdom for such a time as this?" (Esther 4:14, KJV)

"Mordecai taught Queen Esther an essential lesson when he spoke those words. He wanted her to realize that God had given her an opportunity to be a blessing. Now, it wasn't given to her so she could brag about the nobility of which she became a part. God isn't interested in human grandeur. When He allows us to ascend into the clouds, it is only so we can stop the rain with the enlightenment we gained from the laborious progression of our own experiences. Mordecai showed Esther that God had been grooming her all her life for this moment. In spite of the tremendous challenge set before her, she was woman for the job. She was God's choice, a handmaiden fitly chosen and wonderfully endowed for the acquisition of a victorious report."[7]

Bishop T.D. Jakes
Can You Stand To Be Blessed
Treasure House

[7]Jakes, Bishop T.D. *Can You Stand to Be Blessed?* Shippensburg: Treasure House, 1994, pgs. 163-164.

CHAPTER 1

An African American Christian Nation

An African American
Christian Nation

THE AFRICAN AMERICANS, living on the soil of these United States of America, are the only people on the face of the earth who are not recognized as a nation nor belonging to a nation. This great error and injustice must be corrected.

There are distinct blessings from God which are bestowed upon a people when they recognize themselves as a nation. In the divine call to nationhood, God provides corporate blessings that override selfishness and empty personal ambitions. Within this corporate blessing of being a nation, God's provisions can be found from generation to generation. This plan of nations enables God to demonstrate that He is a covenant-keeping God to a thousand generations.

The first step for African Americans to achieve nationhood is to dismiss the perception that they must own a certain portion of the earth to be a nation. Stewardship and not ownership is the greater principle to be in operation. It is important to understand that land occupancy has much to do with the development of heritage and culture. Equally important, it must be understood that both heritage and culture should be perpetuated in the absence of land ownership. In this determination, a people may be forced from their land by an oppressor, but never conquered of their heritage and culture. No military aggression or social assimilation can destroy the identity of a people who ascribe to being a nation. A nation can thrive under great adversity, when the people are cognizant of who they are in the unity of their design.

Nations are called of God to be a blessing to other people. It is God's chosen manner of keeping over five billion inhabitants of His earth functioning with the various location of resources. Where the earth resources end, human resources abound. This factor raises the necessity of every people realizing their need to be a nation. What may be lacking in physical land ownership God more than adequately supplies in creativity and revelation. This allows the Word of God to stand true throughout the ages, *"...he who had gathered much had no excess, and he who had gathered little had no lack...." (Exodus 16:18, NASB)*

In God's covenant relationship with Abraham, God decided that Abraham would be a nation. When Abraham became a nation, he would then be a blessing to others. *"And I will make of thee a great na-*

tion, and I will bless thee, and make thy name great; and thou shalt be a blessing." (Genesis 12:2, KJV) Again, God wishing to display through His friendship with Abraham that nations are to be blessings to others said, *"Seeing that Abraham shall surely become a great and mighty nation, all the nations of the earth shall be blessed in him?"* (Genesis 18:18, KJV) The accomplishments of African Americans have been interpreted and regulated as individual achievements rather than corporate contributions to the cultures and societies of other nations. Yet the corporate blessings proceeding from the African Americans as a nation remains untapped. The Divine principle of nations being a blessing to other nations has not been enacted. The African American Christian Nation is a gift from God awaiting the opportunity to be a blessing to many nations.

The Hebrew word for nation used in both Genesis 12:2 and 18:18 is **gowy.** It means inhabitant, populace, people, tribe, nation; the non-Israelitic peoples. It is a general word used to refer to nations at large, particularly Gentiles (as distinguished from Jews). *Most scholars now believe that the basic idea of* **gowy** *is a defined group of people or a large segment of a given body which is defined by context.* The African American Christian Nation may never be embraced by all African Americans; however, that would not minimize its validity. The truth of the divine principle would operate through a large segment or a remnant segment of a given body! What is the context which defines a specific body in the definition of **gowy?** Nations were defined politically, ethnically, and territorially!

The cure for the multiplicity of sinister offenses found in African American people is in nationhood. *"Righteousness exalteth a nation: but sin is a reproach to any people."* *(Proverbs 14:34, KJV)* The corporate blessing needed to reverse the multiple negativism is in the people arising to become the African American Christian Nation. It is amazing that God never mentioned that Abraham would have to conquer existing nations or subdue other kingdoms to be a nation. African Americans must remove from their thought patterns the imagery of conquering or possessing the land of others before nationhood can be appreciated. God's ways are truly not the ways of man.

What then is the avenue to the establishing of the African American Christian Nation? Spiritual and cultural rebirth mark the beginning. The spiritual rebirth, acceptance of Jesus Christ as Lord and Savior, assures the citizenship which also sets the laws by which the nation shall experience governance. Cultural rebirth is the awareness of a united identity and the conscious choice of being defined as a nation. What follows is an enactment of physical steps to care for one another and preparation to be a blessing to others. The healing that comes to the smaller group will be the blessing for the greater numbers. *"Blessed is the nation whose God is the Lord: and*

*the people whom he hath chosen for his own inherit-
ance." (Psalm 33:12, KJV)*

**Because it has not been does not mean that it
shall not be!** The African American Christian Nation must move forward with the precision planning
that will restore the fortunes of a displaced people
without the claim to nationhood. The steps to freedom are clearly defined: ethical, political, and terri-
torial. God does not cease His program because we
fail to hear Him speak to us.

> *"When he giveth quietness, who then can
> make trouble? and when he hideth his face,
> who then can behold him? whether it be done
> against a nation, or against a man only: That
> the hypocrite reign not, lest the people be en-
> snared."* (Job 34:29,30, KJV)

The birth of the African American Christian Nation is not an issue where place is given to the devil
or doubt. It is a walk by faith and not by sight. It
goes against all that is comfortable. It calls for the
genius of God to be revealed in the creativity of a
people. The comfort zone mentality must be dyna-
mited! The system always seeks homeostasis. But
God! He knows just how and when to break into the
agenda and affairs of men!

> *"Who hath heard such a thing? who hath
> seen such a thing? Shall the earth be made to*

bring forth in one day? or shall a nation be born at once? for as soon as Zion travailed, she brought forth her children." (Isaiah 66:8, KJV)

The answer to the lawlessness running deep and rampant in the African American community is the humbling to the high call of God upon the people. A nation cannot function without the knowledge of God. It is time for African Americans to know God as never before.

"Gather yourselves together, yea, gather together, O nation not desired; before the decree bring forth, before the day pass as the chaff, before the fierce anger of the Lord come upon you, before the day of the Lord's anger come upon you. Seek ye the Lord, all ye meek of the earth, which have wrought his judgment; seek righteousness, seek meekness: it may be ye shall be hid in the day of the Lord's anger." (Zephaniah 2:1-3, KJV)

It is time for new wine to be poured into new wineskins. The time has passed for new agendas to be forced fed into old arenas. In this work, a movement is being launched and not just a mere theory introduction. This is a call to work creatively toward a new vision.

"So shall he sprinkle many nations; the kings shall shut their mouths at him: for that which had not been told them shall they see; and that which they had not heard shall they consider." (Isaiah 52:15, KJV)

This is definitely a call that everyone may not be able to answer. Let him who has an ear hear what the Spirit is saying to the church in this hour. Above all, if you cannot see or commit to the vision, do not allow the devil to use you as a snare or one who blinds others!

CHAPTER 2

From Oppression to Nationhood

From Oppression to Nationhood

THE UNITED STATES SUPREME COURT ruled in March 6, 1857, that Dred Scott was a slave and not a man; therefore, he could not be a citizen of the United States.

"...a U.S. Supreme Court decision which said, in the case of Dred Scott [1857], that no black could be a U.S. citizen and that black people had no rights in America that white people were bound to respect. The net effect of all this was the de facto national-ization of the slave system."[8]

Lerone Bennet, Jr., *Before the Mayflower*,
Fifth Revised Edition

This nation was never designed to include African Americans in ways other than a cheap labor pool or sordid pleasure to morbid minds.

---

[8]Bennett, Jr., Lerone. *Before the Mayflower.* Chicago: Johnson Publishing Company, 1976, pg. 178.

"*The Kansas-Nebraska Act persuaded many antislavery leaders that political action was necessary to combat the relentless drive of the proslavery forces to extend slavery. Northern Whigs, Free Soilers, and Democrats who had fought the passage of the act came together, and out of their discussions arose the Republican party. This new political organization, unalterably antislavery in its point of view, profited by the mistake of earlier antislavery parties and evolved a program broad enough to attract voters who were indifferent to slavery. Southerners, meanwhile, sought to counteract this new party by demanding further extension of slavery and the reopening of the African slave trade.*

"*The significance of these trends had hardly become apparent when the Supreme Court, in 1857, handed down a decision in the case of Scott vs. Sanford that had the effect of widening the breach between North and South. Dred Scott was a Missouri slave whose master had first taken him to live in free Illinois and subsequently to a fort in the northern part of the Louisiana purchase, where slavery had been excluded by the Missouri Compromise. Upon his return to Missouri, Scott sued for his freedom on the ground that residence on free soil had liberated him. The majority of the Court held that Scott was not a citizen and therefore could not bring suit in the courts. Chief Justice Roger B. Taney, speaking for the Court, added that since the Missouri Compromise was unconstitutional, masters could take their slaves anywhere in the territories and retain title to them. The decision was a clear-cut victory for the South, and the North viewed it with genuine alarm. With the highest court in the land openly preaching the proslavery doctrine, there was little hope that anything short of a most drastic political or social revolution would bring an end to slavery.*"[9]

John Hope Franklin
From Slavery to Freedom

God is a covenant keeping God. He covenanted with men to be free and multiply into nations. In fact, God used the slavery exile in Egypt to multiply Israel into a nation. God is the same yesterday, today, and forever. He has used the slavery system of America to multiply African Americans to reach nationhood status. It is now time for the people to whom it is due to walk therein.

Even though Sarah and Abraham got impatient in their awaiting the promised son, God remained faithful to His established principles. Hagar, Sarah's maid, gave birth to Ishmael, Abraham's son. Ishmael was not the son of promise, but God still saw the nations contained in the loins of Ishmael. *"Arise, lift up the lad, and hold him by the hand; for I will make a great nation of him." (Genesis 21:18, NASB)* In fact, God made twelve nations to come forth from

---

[9]Franklin, John Hope. *From Slavery to Freedom.* New York: Alfred A. Knopf, Inc., 1988, pgs. 196 and 262.

Ishmael.

God deals in nations. Nation assignments are of the Lord. *"And He made from one [blood], every nation of mankind to live on all the face of the earth, having determined their appointed times, and the boundaries of their habitation."* *(Acts 17:26, NASB)* God has determined the biological make up of all people. He has appointed the time for them to arise to nationhood status. The Lord God Almighty sets the boundaries of the nations. With the fall of communism, many nations have now returned to autonomy and the borders are reinstated. The reunification of Germany was simply God's statement that He alone establishes the boundaries of nations.

The Catholics have acted on the divine principle of nationhood. The pope operates from his headquarters in the Vatican, an autonomous nation. African Americans must begin asking the question, why not the African American Christian Nation?

It is written, *"Seeing that Abraham shall surely become a great and mighty nation, and all the nations of the earth shall be blessed in him?"* *(Genesis 18:18, KJV)* All people are ordained of God to be a nation. This point cannot be over stressed to the African American people. There are certain blessings that can only come to a people when they function as a nation. There are spiritual laws governing the birth of the African American Christian Nation; therefore, it can only come forth through the church! When Jesus returns, it is recorded, *"And before him them one from another, as a shepherd divideth his sheep from the goats." (Matthew 25:32, KJV)* **The African American Christian Nation must be declared unashamedly and without inhibitions!**

"O Lord, great is Your faithfulness, plenteous in mercy to them that love You, and to them that keep Your commandments. We, as a people, have sinned. We have committed iniquity, have done wickedly, have rebelled, even departing from Your precepts and from Your judgments. Neither have we listened unto Your servants the prophets. We are a people who have no king. Our princes imitate those who oppress and spoil us.

"O Lord, righteousness belongs unto You, but unto us confusion of faces. O Lord, to us belong confusion of faces, we are a people without a king. Our princes do not plead our cause. Our princes seek steadfastedly to become a part of the ruling class and the existing status quo. All our princes are as the princes of the oppressor, they seek after mammon and none stand on Your Holy Word, O God."[10]

Mark C. Olds
Words of Liberation From Prison, 1985

---

[10]Olds, Mark C., *Words of Liberation From Prison,* 1985, pg. 31.

CHAPTER 3

Declaration of Nationhood

Declaration of Nationhood

"*THE SAME AS THE Jewish nation, the African American Christian Nation simply wishes to exercise the right to be obedient to all that God has given as instruction to follow in governing ourselves. Insurrection or the propaganda to overthrow existing orders is not a part of the African American Christian Nation's purpose, plan, or goal. It is a desire to be in position to receive all the blessings which God has intended for this people.*"[11]

Pastor Mark C. Olds
Covenant Gathering Christian Church
Cleveland, Ohio, 1994

All African Americans have the right to be free from bondage, however induced. God designed man with the intent of man enjoying freedom from the beginning. He also designated man to be fruitful

---

[11]An excerpt from a sermon by Mark C. Olds preached at Covenant Gathering Christian Church (Church of God), Cleveland, Ohio, 1994.

and multiply. This multiplication was to emerge into nations. It does not matter that one people's multi- plication process took longer than others, the result is still a nation. It does not matter that the time line of a people's appearance upsets the plan of others, the result is still that a nation has to be born. That which is birthed in the spirit realm shall come forth. Every people have the God mandate to be free and to be a nation!

God also stated very clearly, *"you shall surely set a king over you whom the Lord your God chooses, one from among your countrymen you shall set as king over yourselves; you may not put a foreigner over yourselves who is not your countryman."* *(Deuteronomy 17:15, NASB)* The blessings of the Lord come with obedience. The curses come with disobedience. Blessings overtake the people in obe- dience.

African Americans must obey God and be a na- tion. African Americans must obey God and have a leader from among their own brothers and sisters. It is God's design for people to arise to nationhood sta- tus and have one of their own to rule over them.

> *"Rescue me, and deliver me out of the hand of aliens, Whose mouth speaks deceit, And whose right hand is a right hand of falsehood. Let our sons in their youth be as grown-up plants, And our daughters as corner pillars fashioned as for a palace; Let our garners be*

full, furnishing every kind of produce, And our flocks bring forth thousands and ten thousands in our fields; Let our cattle bear, Without mishap and without loss, Let there be no outcry in our streets! How blessed are the people who are so situated; How blessed are the people whose God is the Lord!" (Psalm 144:11-15, NASB)

It is time to obey God, to be a nation and prosper!

When someone rules over you who is not your brother or sister or a member of your own nation, that nation is in disobedience to God! In nationhood, African Americans will have the opportunity to show, produce and develop among themselves loyalty, discipline, commitment, community, strength, and worship.

CHAPTER
4

Declaration of
Freedom

Declaration of Freedom

" *WHEN JUSTICE IS ABSENT, the social condition and moral condition of any people or nation dips into deep depravity.*"[12]

Mark C. Olds
Understanding the Doctrine of Justice

Freedom brings harmonious living and the practice of justice. Justice is a foundation stone for the African American Christian Nation. Justice cannot be fully comprehended until the spiritual eye of man has freedom.

First of all, justice is a call to the sinner. Justice recognizes the need for evangelism. Justice cannot be fully implanted in the spirit of the person who has not been born again. Evil men cannot comprehend that it is more profitable to love than to exploit. It is the blood washed child of the King (an assiduous

---

[12]Olds, Mark C., *Understanding the Doctrine of Justice,* 1991, pg. 11.

seeker of the Lord's face), who comes away with the revelation knowledge of the doctrine of justice and the grace to understand the dispensation of justice.

African Americans must practice justice among their own nation, and then will other nations be compelled to extend justice in their dealings with this nation. Jesus has approved of African Americans being a nation.

> *"Ye are they which have continued with me in my temptations. And I appoint unto you a kingdom, as my Father hath appointed unto me."* (Luke 22:28,29, KJV)

No other people have endured the wrath of so many other nations, and yet have stood fast in Jesus as African Americans. Through many years of oppression and brutality in its most ugly and racist forms, African Americans have continually called upon the name of Jesus. If any people qualify to be a nation based on what Jesus said, it is African Americans.

The blood of Jesus has brought African Americans into the place to be heirs of God. African Americans must see the need for freedom and self-rule, and submit to Jesus' plan for African Americans. When the plan of Jesus is clearly seen, the people can then grasp hold of the promise of the African American Christian Nation.

Jesus came that man may have abundant temporal life — freedom from injustice — and eternal life — freedom from confining mortality. God wants His creation to enjoy freedom now. If it means loosening the shackles on a nation, God wants His man to have freedom.

No political system, racist society, nor economic caste system can deny freedom to the nation submitted to God; neither can it be denied that that which cries from the depth of man for freedom is in his spirit. God is a spirit. God hears the cry of the spirit of His man. He hears the cry of a nation. He transcends the boundary walls — physical or psychological — established by other men to structure enslavement of other human beings. No matter the extent of physical brutality or sadistic emotional abuse, the spirit of man or a nation can find liberty to rise above the most evil form of oppression by faith in God.

The spirits of bigotry, racism, hatred, prejudice, or any other power of darkness cannot keep out the Spirit of love. The spirits of insouciance and impoverishment must loose their torment of the soul opened to the illumination of the Spirit of love. *"Now the Lord is the Spirit; and where the Spirit of the Lord is, there is liberty."* *(2 Corinthians 3:17, NASB)* The declaration of freedom for the African American Christian Nation is rooted in the truth that it is not God's will that any soul should perish!

SECTION TWO

What Is the Pillar for the Nation?

"And hath made of one blood all nations of men for to dwell on all the face of the earth, and hath determined the times before appointed, and the bounds of their habitation." (Acts 17:26, KJV)

"From the seventy nations that came from the three sons of Noah have come the one hundred and fifty or so nations we have today. Many times, emperors, kings, and councils have decided to form artificial nations that crossed the ancient borders God established on the basis of language, families, and divinely ordained nations. Countless wars have risen from the friction and dislocation that stemmed from man's presumptuous 'rework' of God's original social plan."[13]

Luther Blackwell
The Heritage Of The Black Believer
Treasure House

---

[13]Blackwell, Jr. Luther J., *The Heritage of the Black Believer.* Shippensburg: Treasure House, 1993, pg. 70.

CHAPTER
5

Truth as a
Foundation

Truth as a Foundation

THE AFRICAN AMERICAN CHRISTIAN NA-
TION will bring forth truth as a foundation for building. Truth is not an option when building for the
good of a people. Truth cannot be compromised
when God is the source of supply for an aspiring
nation.

> *"For we can do nothing against the truth,
> but only for the truth."* (2 Corinthians 13:8,
> NASB)

Truth is the only liberating factor! That which
will eliminate false hope and provide a secure future
must be proclaimed.

> *"And you shall know the truth, and the truth
> shall make you free."* (John 8:32, NASB)

Building on any foundation other than the truth
is sinking sand! Truth will enable all people to ar-

ticulate the meaning and reasoning behind the birth of the African American Christian Nation. The unique blend of the spiritual and the cultural, intertwined with the practical development of communication skills and personal interaction (community and individual), will produce the following positives:

- *Increased Self-Esteem and Self-Concept*

Too many African Americans are disillusioned about their personal identity and self-worth. Harmonizing spiritual and cultural references reassures individuals of their ability to achieve. It is also a support mechanism. *"I can do all things through Him who strengthens me." (Philippians 4:13, NASB)*

When the proper perspective of who one really is, is fully realized, the issue of being a part of a nation ceases to be a question. It only stands to reason that poor self-esteem would be advocated by forces which would prohibit people from emerging into a nation.

- *Information on Economic Contributions of African Americans: Local, National, and in the Global Economy*

African Americans are making major contributions to the economic scene in ways other than being entertainers or athletes. Scores of African Americans have obtained MBA's. These brilliant minds are helping to secure stability and profits for numerous multinational corporations. The role of African Americans in the economic arena is not tokenism. There is quality leadership from private entrepreneurship to creative support in major corporation. The ability to develop an economic outreach locally, nationally, and internationally has already been defined. *"Commit your works to the Lord, And your plans will be established. "* (Proverbs 16:3, NASB)

• *Techniques and Social Skills Required to Impact Cross-Cultural Interactions, Ethnicities, and International Interfacing*

The arrest of callous individualism will allow nationalism to take root in the growth of young minds. Corporate gains will be sought rather than individual accolades.

"Our barns will be filled with every kind of provision. Our sheep will increase by thousands, by tens of thousands in our fields; our oxen will draw heavy loads. There will be no breaching of walls, no going into captivity, no cry of distress in our streets. Blessed are the people of whom this is true; blessed are the people whose God is the Lord. " (Psalm 144:13-15, NIV)

Manipulation has no place when a Godly impact is sought rather than worldly recognition. It is no longer enough to merely get along, but a Godly impact must be made which will produce change. Personal acceptance must relinquish its grip on a people focused on the purpose and intent of a nation's birth. This event will unfold techniques and social skills prepared by God in order to produce a Godly impact as opposed to social networking.

• *Understanding the Skills Necessary to Start-Up and Maintain a Nation*

The masterful maintenance of other systems by the intellect and knowledge of African Americans is more than credible to start up and maintain a nation. It is a biblical principle that you should not obtain your own until you have proven faithful over that which belongs to another.

> *"He who is faithful in a very little thing is faithful also in much; and he who is unrighteous in a very little thing is unrighteous also in much. If therefore you have not been faithful in the use of unrighteous mammon, who will entrust the true riches to you? And if you have not been faithful in the use of that which is another's, who will give you that which is your own?"* (Luke 16:10-12, NASB)

African Americans have proven their faithfulness. They have shed their blood in every war involving America.

*"One result of the social and cultural strivings was the emergence of a substantial number of blacks who gave numerous evidences of intellectual growth and of a satisfactory assimilation in American life. This growth was notably reflected in the literary activity of the period. In history and biography there was a tendency, so generally characteristic of the writing of the time, to portray heroic deeds and dramatic successes. In his **The Colored Cadet at West Point (1889)** Henry Ossian Flipper told of his experiences in becoming the first Negro to receive a commission from the United States Military Academy. In 1881 Frederick Douglas brought his colorful career up to date in **The Life and Times of Frederick Douglas**, which was enlarged in 1892.*

"...Negroes performed all kinds of services in the Union army. Organized into raiding parties, they were sent through Confederate lines to destroy fortifications and supplies. Since they knew the Southern countryside better than most white soldiers and could pass themselves off as just another slave, they were extensively used as spies and scouts. White officers relied upon information secured by Negro spies. Harriet Tubman was a spy for Union troops at many points on the eastern seaboard."[14]

John Hope Franklin
From Slavery to Freedom

---

[14]Franklin, John Hope. *From Slavery to Freedom.* New York: Alfred A. Knopf, Inc., 1988, pgs. 196 and 262.

They have given their minds to inventing machinery to advance America's industrial progress. African Americans have accepted every role assigned them in America from slave to statesman and has excelled in commitment and loyalty.

- *Understanding the Skills Necessary to Start Up and Maintain a Business*

African Americans have to become aggressive in business ownership. Preparation for business ownership must become a basic course for our young minds. Desegregation is the single most successful thief of businesses from the African American people. The Negro Baseball League is an excellent illustration of this point. The Negro Baseball League had its own stadiums, team owners, and venders. An economic way of life and social structure for many was destroyed. For the opportunity to attend a major league baseball game, the African Americans forfeited an entire economic base in the exchange. Many other such economic lifelines were lost with the absorption of desegregation. Desegregation was needed, but there was no plan to counter the economic drain of African American businesses.

The attention must turn to launching African American businesses.

"Go to the ant, O sluggard, Observe her ways and be wise, Which, having no chief, Officer or ruler, Prepares her food in the sum-

mer, And gathers her provision in the harvest."
(Proverbs 6:6-8, NASB)

It is a very important and crucial time for African Americans to build and maintain businesses.

• *The Valuable, Tangible Involvement in International Trade (Importing and Exporting)*

African Americans must be energetic in international trade. Restrictions to community business ventures must not be the limit of economic focus or practice. *"For wisdom is protection just as money is protection. But the advantage of knowledge is that wisdom preserves the lives of its possessors." (Ecclesiastes 7:12, NASB)* African Americans have more to offer than a fertile consumer field for global merchants. In this vast field of wealth, there must be a place for sharing in the import and export deficit between African Americans and the rest of the world.

• *The Mindset of a Producer Versus the Mindset of a Consumer Only*

Producers are not complacent to await the next onslaught of consumer goods to take away resources. Producers are creative. They look for ways and means to gain products for reproduction to extend their resources. A consumer does not seek to enrich his resources, but merely seeks to grasp momentary pleasures as a possession.

"And that slave who knew his master's will and did not get ready or act in accord with his will, shall receive many lashes, but the one who did not know it, and committed deeds worthy of a flogging, will receive but few. And from everyone who has been given much shall much be required; and to whom they entrusted much, of him they will ask all the more." (Luke 12:47,48, NASB)

A producer is aware that an investment is necessary and not a leisure option. With production comes the attitude of being responsible to and for others. Out of obedience to God comes a blessing to share with others as the attitude of sower is practiced above the attitude of eater.

"The Lord will command the blessing upon you in your barns and in all that you put your hand to, and He will bless you in the land which the Lord your God gives you....The Lord will open for you His good storehouse, the heavens, to give rain to your land in its season and to bless all the work of your hand; and you shall lend to many nations, but you shall not borrow. And the Lord shall make you the head and not the tail, and you only shall be above, and you shall not be underneath, if you will listen to the commandments of the Lord your God, which I charge you

day, to observe them carefully." (Deuteronomy 28:8; 12,13, NASB)

To exercise the role of the head rather than the tail, a consumer approach must be replaced with a producer mentality.

• *The Spiritual Maturity to Never Again Be Enslaved by Men or Doctrines*

> *"It was for freedom that Christ set us free; therefore keep standing firm and do not be subject again to a yoke of slavery."* (Galatians 5:1, NASB)

African Americans have to retain their freedom through spiritual maturity and a covenant relationship with God. Doctrines as determined by men and women can rob a soul of all that Christ died for in an individual's life. Bondage robs an individual of the freedom to fulfill the destiny which God has already established as potential. The African American Christian Nation will bring forth the continual burning for inner emancipation as planted by Christ.

African Americans must divorce the thought that a nation cannot exist without a land mass. This is not so. A people bonded together politically, ethically, and doing the same economic agenda can arise as a mighty nation. The land was decreed after the Emancipation Proclamation. Remember? Forty acres and a mule. Although decreed by the U.S. Congress, there was never a legal avenue legislated to enforce the substance decree. This was not a slip of careless legislators. It was deliberate. The forty acres and a mule was more than giving a wronged segment of the population a small token to begin life. Such a massive release of land would have granted nationhood status for the freed Negro. These legislators were bound by the mindset that land was essential for nationhood. They likewise propagandized this teaching, but now that school of thought is irrelevant. **Truth is the foundation for the birth of a nation!**

CHAPTER
6

Economic
Focus

Economic Focus

THE AFRICAN AMERICAN CHRISTIAN NATION has a very definite economic focus. The primary goal of the African American Christian Nation is to provide information, instruction, and the practical opportunity to a consumer base of thirty million African Americans. It is to make economics both applicable and profitable in a nonexploitative manner — retaining moral values, cultural awareness, and spiritual maturity in an autonomous fashion.

Practical economics will be a vital part of building the African American Christian Nation. To be a successful and viable vehicle for the African American community to emerge as a nation, there must be a prayerful and insightful look into its current economic conditions. Special attention must be placed on entrepreneurial opportunities (or the lack thereof) for African American youth and young adults. There is an obvious need for a resource pool to develop new businesses and ownership of highly used products in the African American community. There is little opportunity for mentorship experience when there are so few businesses in the community that are actually owned by African Americans. There is a need for an influx of capital into the African American community to be controlled by African Americans who reside in the neighborhoods. This is really key to the growth of the African American Christian Nation.

To awaken the great concentration of resources within the African American people and bring salvation to this great multitude, a shocking truth is needed to bring about the desire to understand. **African Americans have been historically raped and are contemporarily raped as a result of continuous oppression (drugs, alcohol, poverty, disease, oppression, illiteracy).** African Americans must be seen as more than a target population for the next marketing craze. The African American Christian Nation will give a voice to those who have become disenfranchised and excluded from the democratic process. The African American Christian Nation will enhance the academic and creative ability of the *(pronounced)* expendable multitude while strengthening their mental, cultural, and spiritual foundation.

Most significantly, the African American Christian Nation will establish a sound economic base in order to expand the horizons of the minds of youthful African Americans. The economic development component is a strong and pertinent attempt to inter-vene and counter the pressures that place African American youth (rural area or inner city) at risk for drug abuse, school dropout, and gang violence.

Along with training and implementation, the African American Christian Nation will be able to perpetually serve the people culturally, morally, and spiritually. A decisive effort by the African Ameri-can Christian Nation will be a valuable economic venture across multiple geographic settings. When an initial strong economic base is established, other consumer areas will be opened. For example, Afri-can Americans spend hundreds of millions of dol-lars on athletic shoes each year. These *footwear* prod-ucts, for the most part, are sold in stores in the United States for as much as $200 per pair. If African Ameri-cans were able to manufacture this same footwear in a country on the continent of Africa, it would help descendants of their ancestors as well as reduce the high exploitation of the people of color living in these United States. **African Americans must recognize and understand clearly the struggle for economic, cultural, spiritual, and national identity.**

The African American Christian Nation sends a message that African Americans can no longer be viewed as consumers only. The people of the Afri-can American community deserve an opportunity to become producers in their own community. If an industry such as the soft drink industry can make hundreds of millions of dollars annually from the

African American community, it should be willing to invest an equitable share of those profits to the economic development of the youth and young adults of that community. The soft drink giants had no difficulty running to invest billions in Russia and other former communist nations. The soft drink giants ran to invest in a partnership with other nations with a great potential profit return. African Americans must grow up from being labeled a community to being recognized as a nation!

All African Americans should abstain from all soft drinks for a ninety-day period. The makers of the syrup which is shipped across this nation would want to know the reason why the nonconsumption among the African Americans.

"The economic highway to power has few entry lanes for Negroes. Nothing so vividly reveals the crushing impact of discrimination and the heritage of exclusion as the limited dimensions of Negro business in the most powerful economy in the world. America's industrial production is half of the world's total, and within it the production of Negro business is so small that it can scarcely be measured on any definable scale.

"Yet in relation to the Negro community the value of Negro business should not be underestimated. In the internal life of the Negro society it provides a degree of stability. Despite formidable obstacles it has developed a corps of men of competence and

organizational discipline who constitute a talented leadership reserve. Their cumulative strength may be feeble measured against the mammoth of white industry, but within the community they furnish inspiration and are a resource for the development of programs and planning. They are a strength among the weak, though they are weak among the mighty.

There exists two other areas, however, where Negroes can exert substantial influence on the broader economy. As employees and consumers Negro numbers and their strategic disposition endow them with a certain bargaining strength. "[15]

Rev. Dr. Martin Luther King, Jr.
Where Do We Go From Here:
Chaos or Community?

When their profits would be severely cut, they should be willing to invest in employee ownership of factories making soft drink containers, caps, crates, labels or the like. Regional plants, with employee ownership by African Americans, manufacturing support articles must become a part of the economic base of the community which contributes so heavily to an industry's success. The African American Christian Nation will convey to the soft drink industry (or any industry) that the time has passed for individual appeasement, but a nation is desirous of investments in all its people.

---

[15]King, Jr. Martin Luther. *Where Do We Go From Here: Chaos or Community?* New York: Harper & Row, Publishers, Incorporated, 1968, pgs. 139-140.

This abstinence from all soft drinks will produce an important economic unity among African Americans. This unity will stimulate the growth of personal and corporate esteem. It will reveal the power of unity and the voice economic recognition gives the African American Christian Nation. Abstinence from all soft drinks as an economic campaign will restore identity to the young people involved in its initial thrust. It will connect these young minds with a previous generation of justice fighters who have completed their course and have left an economic justice and nationhood struggle to be won.

To be able to demonstrate an economic impact upon a specific industry in a defined time frame will ensure that this movement is a voice to be heard. Young people making a historical contribution (by active participation) in their lifetime can build upon such achievements for future inspirational ideas for reliable nation building and expansion through non-violent alternatives.

To take the example of abstinence from all soft drinks a step further, the action would send a clear message to the industry that the people are demanding a chance to change the options for the lives of the young people birthed into their community. No longer will the people be satisfied that a few already wealthy or middle class African Americans are granted franchise options or hired in some corporate executive level position. Such an appeasement practice has outlived its value to the growing numbers left behind without an opportunity to positively change their lives. No longer will African Americans be viewed as targets of any industry to increase sales and profits without retribution or profit sharing. **CONSUMER ONLY LABEL** must now be removed from African Americans.

The African American community must rechannel its consumer spending into a major resource. When consumer spending is viewed as a resource, then industries which enjoy hundreds of millions of dollars in profit must be responsible for reinvesting in the community. This is not another appeal for a handout. This is a call for the African American community (especially the youth and young adults) to recognize the value of their buying power. Each step of revelation enables a people to see their value to others as a nation.

The Scriptures produce a great example of a leader not allowing merchants or merchandise to overrun his people. Nehemiah (chapter 13, verses 15-22) refused to allow foreigners to camp outside the gates of Jerusalem to await selling their goods on the Sabbath. The foreign industry had no regard for the spiritual laws of his nation. They viewed the people as consumers. They viewed the Sabbath as another day for profit making. The Prophet Nehemiah stood up for his people and demanded respect for his nation. This necessary respect forced these foreign merchants to remove the stigma and role of consumers only from Nehemiah's nation! The African American Christian Nation must likewise view economics as a part of the spiritual law within its borders. Abstinence from consuming the products of an industry will allow the African American Christian Nation to follow Nehemiah's example. No one will be able to exploit this people any longer. All who wish to trade with this nation must be willing to see a partnership (ownership) become a real exchange.

The people of the African American Christian Nation will gain cultural, spiritual, and economic inroads by defeating the notion of any industry that the people are only to be counted as profit from the industry's latest marketing introduction. Exclusion from economic decisions as relating to the people of the African American Christian Nation will not be acceptable or practical. Inclusion at every level will become an identifiable norm for the industry wishing to count the dollars of the African American Christian Nation in its profit projections!

The need for nationhood is clearly expressed as it changes the approach to daily issues. Areas once viewed as individual or community weakness are seen as the strength of a nation. The African American Christian Nation produces a new thought pattern. These thought patterns are based on God's ability to get glory for Himself out of what seems practically meaningless to man.

"But God has chosen the foolish things of the world to shame the wise, and God has chosen the weak things of the world to shame the

things which are strong, and the base things of the world and the despised, God has chosen, the things that are not, that He might nullify the things that are, that no man should boast before God." (1 Corinthians 1:27-29, NASB)

The economic factor as a stimulator becomes a reference point to provide a fresh infusion for financial development among the people who seek sobriety and peace. The time for the African American Christian Nation has arrived!

Commitment to Unity and Service

Commitment to Unity and Service

WE, THE SAINTS OF THE MOST HIGH GOD, African Americans in ethnicity, and members of the Body of Christ under the Lordship of Jesus Christ, God, the Father's only begotten Son, seek to be willing and obedient to all that is written in the Word of God for us to perform.

We, the African American Christian Nation, do make a commitment to seek unity as a way of life and rendering service to all through the empowerment granted by the Holy Spirit. It is God, Who by one blood has made all nations and set the boundaries of those nations, that African Americans now respond to form a nation whereby our own can govern themselves in accordance to the mandates of God Almighty, the Father of Jesus Christ, our Lord.

The African American Christian Nation, in obedience to God, humbly seeks His guidance upon becoming an example and structure to bring our ethnicity out of chaos, poverty, oppression, sin, and reproach. May God ever grant the African American Christian Nation peace, protection, and prosperity while accepting our praise, exaltation, and worship, in Jesus' name, amen and hallelujah!

UNITY

"Behold, how good and how pleasant it is for brethren to dwell together in unity! It is like the precious ointment upon the head, that ran down upon the beard, even Aaron's beard: that went down to the skirts of his garments; as the dew of Hermon, and as the dew that descended upon the mountains of Zion: for there the Lord commanded the blessing, even life for evermore." (Psalm 133, KJV)

It is good in the eyes of God for brethren to dwell together in unity. Because it seems good to God, the African American brethren have a mandate from God to pursue unity. It is imperative to state that brethren cannot have true unity without nationhood. To exist as a non-nation, African Americans cut themselves off from this very potential. Without a nation, it is every man to his own tent. With that individualized isolation, assimilation into the nationhood (wherever possible) and cultures of others is inevitable. With assimilation into the cultures and societies of other people, divisions arise as a result of choices of who to follow other than your own.

God also finds it pleasant for brethren to enjoy unity. There is peace with unity. The strength to struggle together and overcome obstacles develops unity between brethren pleasant. Development and potential are discovered. Differences between brothers, who are seeking the common ground of advancement for their people, lose the sting of a flame. These differences are then changed into steps to climb and ascend to new heights together.

Unity as defined by Webster means: (1) the state of being one, oneness, singleness; (2) something complete in itself; (3) the quality of being one in spirit, sentiment, purpose; harmony; agreement; concord; uniformity. The African American Christian Nation is calling for the oneness of spirit, purpose, and concord for the people of the same likeness. The Hebrew word for unity in Psalm 133 is **yachad** which means to be or become one, a unit, alike.

Jesus held the same desire for brothers to dwell in unity. He prayed, *"...Holy Father, keep them in Thy name, the name which Thou hast given Me, that they may be one, even as We are."* (John 17:11, NASB) The Psalmist also records a significant promise from God where unity abides, *"...For there the Lord commanded the blessing — life forever."* (Psalm 133:3, KJV) Moving to nationhood is not a time to be fearful. It is a definite act of faith to see a mighty deliverance of a people. God is still the God of the oppressed. God is still doing new things in the earth. It requires faith. Luke's Gospel records these words of Jesus.

"Now shall not God bring about justice for His elect, who cry to Him day and night, and will He delay long over them? I tell you that He will bring about justice for them speedily. However, when the Son of Man comes, will He find faith on the earth?" (Luke 18:7,8, NASB)

SERVICE

"And he said unto them, 'The kings of the Gentiles exercise lordship over them; and they that exercise authority upon them are called benefactors. But ye shall not be so: but he that is greatest among you, let him be as the younger; and he that is chief, as he that doth serve. For whether is greater, he that sitteth at meat, or he that serveth? is not he that sitteth at meat? but I am among you as he that serveth." (Luke 22:25-27, KJV)

The African American Christian Nation is not an escape artist tactic to evade servanthood. In fact, it is the beckoning to the higher call of servanthood: commitment. The word servant triggers reactions among many African Americans. This is understandable because of our experience in America. *To some, servant means to be less than another, inferior. Webster defines servant as a person employed by another, as for domestic work or other labor.* That

turns many people away from wanting to have anything to do with being a servant. *Webster goes further to state a servant to be a slave.* The slave connotation eliminates most African Americans from
even thinking about being a servant to anybody. *One
last definition by Webster for servant, one who ex-
erts himself for the benefit of another, his master;
specifically, an official of a government; as a public
servant.* To be a part of a new nation, African Americans are going to have to practice without a slack
hand exerting themselves for the benefit of others.
It will take humble men and women to build a nation, servants, not ambitious frauds seeking a crown-
ing as a prince or princess. The higher call of
servanthood presents a challenge to any people who
will dare to live holy and escape the shackles of oppression.

> *"Ye call me Master and Lord: and ye say
> well; for so I am. If I then, your Lord and
> Master, have washed your feet; ye also ought
> to wash one another's feet. For I have given
> you an example, that ye should do as I have
> done to you."* (John 13:13-15, KJV)

Jesus was pretty clear in His statements to the disciples. I am Lord and Master. I have chosen to be a
servant. I wash your feet as an example of how
people are to serve one another no matter what their
position. Even a position is a tool of servanthood, it
is not to be used to flaunt or promote one's self.

To serve is defined by Webster as: (1) to execute the requirements of an office; (2) to answer a purpose; (3) to be usable as a substitute; (4) in a religious sense, to obey and to worship, as to serve God; (5) to benefit, help, or promote; (6) love. When a need is visible, a servant responds as a requirement to the office occupied. A servant arrives with a purpose in mind, to be used as a substitute for the one in need. A servant is always looking for a way to love someone or be of benefit to another.

Those who serve work to see a unit become a reality. They have no problem worshipping and obeying God in whatever He requires. They love to serve. Servants realize that in order for the African American Christian Nation to become a reality, there must be a unit of servers. A group working together for a common purpose must arise. A people seeking nationhood must have a required purpose and be willing to organize for that particular purpose.

Unity and service will lead a people into the blessings which God has decreed for brethren to enjoy as a nation under God!

CHAPTER
8

Legitimate Governing Apparatus

Legitimate Governing Apparatus

"*NATIONS ARE PEOPLE GROUPS who hold certain things in common. Some nations are great and powerful while others are less dominant. Regardless of the stature, God has instituted the nations. Today when God establishes a nation, He may cause a people to come together from different traditions, different languages, different cultures; but He weaves them together as one integrated community. They have common problems, common difficulties, common hopes and aspirations. So He organizes the world into nations.*"[16]

C.B. Peter Morgan
The Nations, Destiny Image

The African American Christian Nation must formulate and introduce a legitimate governing apparatus to represent the concerns of the previously disempowered and the previously disenfranchised

---

[16]Morgan, C.B. Peter. *The Nations*. Shippensburg: Destiny Image, 1992, pgs. 7-8.

people of African American ethnicity. Also, African Americans, who have realized a degree of acceptance in the corporate structure, must come to grips with the reality that their appearance of success does not exempt them from the struggles of their ethnicity. The African American Christian Nation must be their legitimate government as well.

OLD TESTAMENT EXAMPLE
Exodus 20:2-17

No government can operate without a foundational promise which assures the people of equality and justice. Most governing systems profess the principle of equality and justice for all its citizens in theory. The practice is usually not applied by its leadership or princeship alignment.

The African American Christian Nation must raise a legitimate governing apparatus that is not only utopian in theory, but one which is practical. Such a governmental depiction could only manifest out of relationships. A people willing to live in covenant with God and community.

Before there can be a congress or parliament, there must be a foundation of righteousness and holiness. Justice must flow from the Spirit of God.

"Open your mouth for the dumb, For the rights of all the unfortunate. Open your mouth, judge righteously, And defend the rights of the afflicted and need....It is an abomination for

kings to commit wickedness, For a throne is established on righteousness." (Proverbs 31:8,9 and Proverbs 16:12, NASB)

A commitment to justice is a commitment to God and the people.

REVERENCE FOR GOD
Exodus 20:2-8, NASB

"I am the Lord your God, who brought you out of the land of Egypt, out of the house of slavery. You shall have no other gods before Me. You shall not make for yourself an idol, or any likeness of what is in heaven above or on the earth beneath or in the water under the earth. You shall not worship them or serve them; for I, the Lord your God, am a jealous God, visiting the iniquity of the fathers on the children, on the third and fourth generations of those who hate Me, but showing loving-kindness to thousands, to those who love Me and keep My commandments. You shall not take the name of the Lord your God in vain, for the Lord will not leave him unpunished who takes His name in vain. Remember the sabbath day, to keep it holy."

God demands the preeminence in the lives of His people. Even with the great emphasis on ethnicity, heritage, and culture, biological pride misconstrued can emerge as an idol. Worship is to always be to the true and living God, who alone has brought the people from slavery to nationhood. He is a jealous God who desires undivided affection in worship.

"For I, the Lord, love justice...." (Isaiah 61:8, NASB) The people should always love what God loves. It is clear that God loves justice. *"And I will make justice the measuring-line, And righteousness the level; Then hail shall sweep away the refuge of lies, And the waters shall overflow the secret place."* (Isaiah 28:17, NASB) It is imperative to place God first in establishing the nation. In setting Him first, He can speak and provide navigation for a people through the most tumultuous times. *"Therefore the Lord longs to be gracious to you, And therefore He waits on high to have compassion on you. For the Lord is a God of justice; How blessed are all those who long for Him."* (Isaiah 30:18, NASB) When there is reverence for God, there is a conformity to His character. Arguments are reduced and resources saved, when the governing apparatus does not have to try and legislate a moral standard of living.

RELATIONSHIP WITH FELLOW MAN
Exodus 20:12-17, NASB

"Honor your father and your mother, that your days may be prolonged in the land which the Lord your God gives you. You shall not murder. You shall not commit adultery. You shall not steal. You shall not bear false wit-

ness against your neighbor. You shall not covet your neighbor's house; you shall not covet your neighbor's wife or his male servant or his female servant or his ox or his donkey or anything that belongs to your neighbor."

A nation which honors God will practice respect for parents and elders. The extended family will be valued. A nonviolent life-style reverses the current trend of malicious behavior. Integruous love eliminates immoral relationships. Thievery is removed by people of honesty, who are willing to share and care for others. Truth toward one another dissolves anguish and encourages peace. The removal of envy and jealousy paves the road for collaboration in all phases.

A people mindful of relationship building realizes the value of their brothers and sisters. Within relationships, selfishness and individualism are not the ideal of achievement. The pinnacle of success is measured by the group success when relationship is the higher measuring line. The African American Christian Nation unfolds the ultimate living example of covenant relationships.

NEW TESTAMENT CONFIRMATION
Matthew 5:17-20, NASB

"Do not think that I came to abolish the Law or the Prophets; I did not come to abolish, but to fulfill. For truly I say to you, until

*heaven and earth pass away, not the smallest
letter or stroke shall pass away from the Law,
until all is accomplished. Whoever then an-
nuls one of the least of these commandments,
and so teaches others, shall be called least in
the kingdom of heaven; but whoever keeps and
teaches them, he shall be called great in the
kingdom of heaven. For I say to you, that un-
less your righteousness surpasses that of the
scribes and Pharisees, you shall not enter the
kingdom of heaven."*

The Apostle Paul wrote to the Corinthian Christians regarding the Old Testament writings, *"Now
these things happened as examples for us...."
(1 Corinthians 10:6, NASB)* To establish a new nation, it is needful to look at the example set by God.
Jesus confirms that we should utilize the examples
of the Old Testament. He affirms that His mission is
not to abolish, but to fulfill.

The African American Christian Nation has not
come to set aside the works of other men. On the
contrary, it has come to fulfill within a people what
God has established. God's purpose will be accomplished. The African American Christian Nation
chooses to follow Jesus.

*"I glorified Thee on the earth, having ac-
complished the work which Thou hast given
Me to do."* (John 17:4, NASB)

The rise from disenfranchisement to nationhood will bring glory to God. Anything less than African Americans becoming a nation will not accomplish the work God has assigned to this people.

DUAL CITIZENSHIP
Philippians 3:5, NASB, and Acts 22:25-28, NASB

> *"Circumcised the eighth day, of the nation of Israel, of the tribe of Benjamin, a Hebrew of Hebrews; as to the Law, a Pharisee."*
>
> *"And when they stretched him out with thongs, Paul said to the centurion who was standing by, 'Is it lawful for you to scourge a man who is a Roman and uncondemned?' And when the centurion heard this, he went to the commander and told him, saying, 'What are you about to do? For this man is a Roman.' And the commander came and said to him, 'Tell me, are you a Roman?' And he said, 'Yes.' And the commander answered, 'I acquired this citizenship with a large sum of money.' And Paul said, 'But I was actually born a citizen.'"*

A member of the African American Christian Nation is not required to surrender United States citizenship. The life of the Apostle Paul is an illustration of dual citizenship. He was a Roman citizen, but he was also very much a member of the Jewish nation. He was a high ranking official in Judaism. Of course, Paul also became a citizen of heaven with his conversion to Christianity. A Christian is still a citizen of heaven, even as that individual has become a part of the African American Christian Nation. Saints must always examine the Scriptures to assure themselves that they are in the faith.

CONCLUSION
Matthew 22:37-40, NASB

"And He said to him, 'You shall love the Lord your God with all your heart, and with all your soul, and with all your mind.' This is the great and foremost commandment. And a second is like it, 'You shall love your neighbor as yourself.' On these two commandments depend the whole Law and the Prophets."

The African American Christian Nation has to raise up a people to love God and love and respect one another. This is divine order and protection. The enemy who brings destruction has no channel of entrance when a people love God and their brothers and sisters. The identification motto of the African American Christian Nation must be, *"By this all men will know that you are My disciples, if you have love for one another." (John 13:35, NASB)*

SECTION THREE

How to Enact the Nation

"Commit thy works unto the Lord, and thy thoughts shall be established." (Proverbs 16:3, KJV)

"A genuine revolution of values means in the final analysis that our loyalties must become ecumenical rather than sectional. Every nation must now develop an overriding loyalty to mankind as a whole in order to preserve the best in their individual societies."[17]

Rev. Dr. Martin Luther King, Jr.
Where Do We Go From Here: Chaos or Community?
Beacon

[17]King, Jr. Martin Luther. *Where Do We Go From Here: Chaos or Community?* Boston: Beacon Press, 1968, pg. 190.

CHAPTER
9

Departments of
the Cabinet

Departments of
the Cabinet

THE FOLLOWING DEPARTMENTS will form the cabinet to forge the healing of the people and the propelling of a nation. The light has come to illuminate the path leading from chaos and destruction to peace and prosperity.

1. DEPARTMENT OF HEALTH CARE AND THE ENVIRONMENT

The principles of divine healing are strongly supported and will be unequivocally taught by this department. Yet there remains the tremendous needs of the multitudes who are yet lacking such faith. All people must be included in terms of potential health care needs. A body restored is a candidate for spiritual regeneration.

Of course, prevention education is a vital area of health care. *"Beloved, I pray that in all respects you may prosper and be in good health, just as your soul prospers." (3 John 2, NASB)* The Apostle John wanted his readers to be in good health. The good health of any nation means more resources diverted for enhancement. The greater number of people in good health also translates into a greater number of healthy minds functioning on a creative path. The wholeness of a people adds to the prosperity of that people.

Health care ranks as a high priority, especially among the youth and elderly. Medical clinics staffed with Christian doctors and nurses must be established and strategically placed within the community. Health care has to be accessible for all. Health care and proper diet will promote a stronger mental capacity to digest the Word of God.

The Apostle John wanted for his readers good health in all respects. This means in contemporary times that any people desirous to be a nation must perform its own research. There must be an end to all authorized and unauthorized research on African Americans. Profiteering through medical labs which falsify findings from routine analyst must come to a halt. False findings lead to unnecessary surgery or a life of addiction to prescribed medicines (legalized drug dealerships). In all respects, the African American Christian Nation must labor toward the good health of its people.

The Apostle John also prayed that the readers would prosper. The practical elimination of as many individuals as possible from the welfare rolls as early as possible is of the utmost urgency to the African

American Christian Nation. Poverty is an ugly disease which is often fatal. It is treatable and a family may be immunized against it. *"And let our people also learn to engage in good deeds [occupations] to meet pressing needs, that they may not be unfruitful." (Titus 3:14, NASB)* Healthy people are not unfruitful (naturally or spiritually). Mentally, emotionally, and physically sound people wish to prosper in all respects. It is a burning desire. When this burning desire is present, the words of the Apostle Paul come alive.

> *"Finally then, brethren, we request and exhort you in the Lord Jesus that, as you received from us instruction as to how you ought to walk and please God (just as you actually do walk), that you may excel still more."* (1 Thessalonians 4:1, NASB)

The driving force is the unction to be of greater excellence in all respects of good health and its completeness.

The environment is a part of the care of the African American Christian Nation. The settlements of African Americans must not be the dump sites of toxic wastes. Care of the environment is a responsibility. It is not a concern of people who are opting for a subculture life-style.

> *"For the anxious longing of the creation waits eagerly for the revealing of the sons of*

God. For the creation was subjected to futil-
ity, not of its own will, but because of Him who
subjected it, in hope that the creation itself also
will be set free from its slavery to corruption
into the freedom of the glory of the children of
God. For we know that the whole creation
groans and suffers the pains of childbirth to-
gether until now." (Romans 8:19-22, NASB)

The earth is awaiting for the children of God to stand
in their rightful place that it may find liberation. A
quality environment is essential to good health care.
The environment will not improve until the people
of God understand their responsibility. The African
American Christian Nation will act on behalf of
creation's liberation through this department.

2. DEPARTMENT OF YOUTH AND YOUNG ADULT MOBILIZATION

This department will have the responsibility of
developing programs which stimulates and educates
young people to their value and worth to the African
American Christian Nation. If young people cannot
see their value to their own nation, it is illogical to
think that they will perceive having a merit or value
to others.

"Train up a child in the way he should go,
Even when he is old he will not depart from
it." (Proverbs 22:6, NASB)

Programs must be generated with specifically designed curricula to propel African American young people politically, culturally, and spiritually. Indoctrination by other systems have to be halted in their pollutions of the young minds of the African American populace whether the tactics result from acculturation and misinformation, or disinformation.

It will be this department's responsibility to referendum young people to the importance of their active participation in the development of the nation. *"It is by his deeds that a lad distinguishes himself If his conduct is pure and right."* *(Proverbs 20:11, NASB)* Excellence is an expectancy of all who contribute to the emergence of this nation. All are counted and needed to make wholehearted contributions of all natures. Youth is not to be despised, but called upon to display a distinguishable and beneficial character.

These same young minds must be aware of being accountable and responsible to the African American Christian Nation. *"Remember also your Creator in the days of your youth, before the evil days come and the years draw near when you will say, 'I have no delight in them.'"* *(Ecclesiastes 12:1, NASB)* This department will be a great evangelistic advancement and discipleship enhancement to reach multitudes of young people.

3. DEPARTMENT OF COMMUNICATIONS

> *"Like cold water to a weary soul, So is good news from a distant land."* (Proverbs 25:25, NASB)

The official African American Christian Nation media consortium must arise through this department. This is necessary to preserve an accurate history of our people. The eradication of myths and lies will lead to a greater celebration of peace. *"For lack of wood the fire goes out, And where there is no whisperer, contention quiets down."* (Proverbs 26:20, NASB)

In the midst of abundant negative propaganda and the deluge of half truths, the need for vehicles to set forth an accurate portrayal of the present is essential. *"A good name is to be more desired than great riches, Favor is better than silver and gold."* (Proverbs 22:1, NASB) At the emergence of something new and genuine, the old and pretentious will be exposed and thereby losing its power. Truth in all situations must be proclaimed.

> *"Have I not written to you excellent things Of counsels and knowledge, To make you know the certainty of the words of truth That you may correctly answer to him who sent you?"* (Proverbs 22:20,21, NASB)

The official African American Christian Nation media consortium must assure the people of an accurate articulation of the vision for the future. This vital element of the African American Christian Nation must design and produce a national newspaper, magazine, periodical, radio, television, and cable television network to send forth truth that will dispel any myths formulated against this mission.

This department will likewise serve as the electronic evangelism center. The freedom to publish books and related materials relevant to this people will help shape this nation politically, socially, and theologically.

4. DEPARTMENT OF THE ARTS

This department shall proclaim the creativity of the people without compromising the biblical standard of holiness. *"For the ways of a man are before the eyes of the Lord, And He watches all his paths."* *(Proverbs 5:21, NASB)* Entertainment alone cannot be the sole reason for the arts. It is important to capture the heritage and culture of a people through the eyes of the Lord and the eyes of that people. Any misrepresentation is already under the scrutiny of the Lord. The Lord watches as the heritage and culture of a nation are stolen by others.

The satanic forces are always busy in an attempt to destroy a nation. With the destruction of a nation, the people are consumed by evil and spiritual corruption.

"He who keeps a royal command experiences no trouble, for a wise heart knows the proper time and procedure. For there is a proper time and procedure for every delight, when a man's trouble is heavy upon him. If no one knows what will happen, who can tell him when it will happen? No man has authority to restrain the wind with the wind, or authority over the day of death; and there is no discharge in the time of war, and evil will not deliver those who practice it." (Ecclesiastes 8:5-8, NASB)

The struggle for a clear declaration of a people's heritage and culture is a never-ending warfare. It is a spiritual warfare which has no furlough or cease-fire agreements.

In order to retain purity in the illumination of the arts, the hearts who observe must be pure. The arts have to produce a balm of healing as when David played upon his instrument in the courts of King Saul. The performing arts and the arts produced by the creative flow of the skilled must possess a healing balm for the people. The arts must be recaptured to be an evangelistic tool and a counseling tool. Moral and spiritual issues such as divorce, abortion, incest, rape, and other difficult areas have to be dealt with informatively and spiritually. All aspects of the arts must exemplify reconciliation as works of ambassadors for Christ.

5. DEPARTMENT OF THE AFRICAN EXPATRIATION COMMEMORATED

The responsibility for the assurance of the perpetuation of the official holiday of the African American Christian Nation comes under this department. This holiday is celebrated each year in August. August mirrors the time of the first slaveship's arrival in America at Jamestown, Virginia. The African Expatriation Commemorated is based on the book of Esther and the example of the Feast of Purim. The African Expatriation Commemorated parallels the Feast of Purim as God provided a mighty victory for the Jewish nation. In these contemporary times, He is delivering the African American people by intervening in the systems that oppress and rob them of freedom. God's intervention is bringing this people to being a free nation and an example to those operating in darkness.

The African Expatriation Commemorated is pivotal in the consummation of the spiritual and cultural bond of the people of African descent. The spiritual rebirth delivers meaning to life while the cultural rebirth reorientates the values of life. The African American Christian Nation must retain a true and free cultural renaissance which liberates the heritage and legacy of a people from myths and stereotypes.

African American people need a spiritual rebirth-regeneration, to be the vanguard of the positive re-emergence of a productive state. "Spiritual and Cultural Rebirth" instill meaning to a people who have not enjoyed the benefit of social and cultural autonomy.

The events marking this holiday would be centered upon the heritage and legacy of people of African descent. A holiday to recognize the death and brutality experienced throughout the **African Expatriation** (historically factual) serves to enlighten all people of a great human rights violation. This time of remembrance is designed to be a declaration to all people of African descent to recall a crippling factor in the non-evolution of African people into a major role in the shaping of world policy. This memorial is established in the spirit of resurrection instead of lamentation. **THE AFRICAN EXPATRIATION COMMEMORATED** mandates all African Americans to realize their full potential as a people in the global village. The recall of heritage and legacy calls African descendants to strength and love.

This holiday will ignite unity within a people. It will provide young people the profound inner-emancipation of having made a historical contribution in their lifetime. This will serve as a catalyst for future inspirational ideas for reliable development and expansion of a people. African American people will gain cultural and spiritual unity. The stigma of an uncertain past will be changed into a positive enlightenment. Nationalistic fervor evolves from this demonstration of loyalty.

The spiritual and cultural value of such a holiday is invaluable and immeasurable. The unity requirement surrounding the African Expatriation Commemorated uplifts African descendants to greater self-determination in overcoming obstacles. A reference point is established to provide a fresh infusion of harmonious living (sobriety and peace) within the African American Christian Nation.

6. DEPARTMENT OF MISSIONARIES

This department has the responsibility of advancing the Kingdom of God by spreading the Gospel of Jesus Christ. This department has the responsibility of establishing New Testament Church practices and life in urban settings as well as rural scenarios.

"And Jesus came and spake unto them, saying, 'All power is given unto me in heaven and in earth. Go ye therefore, and teach all nations, baptizing them in the name of the Father, and of the Son, and of the Holy Ghost: Teaching them to observe all things whatsoever I have commanded you: and, lo, I am with you alway, even unto the end of the world.' Amen." (Matthew 28:18-20, KJV)

"And he said unto them, 'It is not for you to know the times or the seasons, which the Father hath put in his own power. But ye shall receive power, after that the Holy Ghost is come upon you: and ye shall be witnesses unto

me both in Jerusalem, and in all Judaea, and in Samaria, and unto the uttermost part of the earth.'" (Acts 1:7,8, KJV)

To take this Gospel to every nation, saints must have a starting point. The witness commences in your geographical locale. The greatest potential for witnessing is outside of the sanctuary. A corp of doctrinally sound saints needs to witness daily from door to door. These are the "foot soldiers of God." Their mission is to take the Gospel to the unchurched.

Reaching the unchurched requires a strategy. It must be a wholistic approach to the multiple problems people face today. This is a major step in the recovery of lives on an individual basis with a multi-optional approach. To enhance the ministry, there must be an application of an evangelistic witness, informational provisions, spiritual guidance, and the practical opportunity to make positive strides while gaining moral values, cultural awareness, and spiritual maturity.

This department must create activities which are designed to produce a Christian environment, to provide alternative information and decision-making skills necessary for youth and young adults to select actions that are legal, short-term, rewarding and a source of self-esteem. To effectively develop Christian bases, the missionaries (servers of the Gospel) must be eager and able to provide social, cultural, and spiritual programs which will empower disenfranchised people.

Missionaries (servers of the Gospel) will be called upon to witness to all people (young and old) and bring them into an arena whereby discipleship can take place. As the discipleship process unfolds, the natural skill level is also cultivated. Missionaries are designated "foot soldiers" with a mission to counter the brightest young minds from pursuing a career in illegal drug sales and distribution.

The moral truth set forth by the church remains the stability of the people in tumultuous times. People who do not know Jesus must come to understand their rich potential and the covenant (promise) of God. When people are made to understand their citizenship in heaven and the requirement to live in harmony on earth, they will understand the need to stop the plight of submitting to acts which lead to demoralized lives.

7. DEPARTMENT OF FOOD DISTRIBUTION

Food distribution is an essential start to any program geared toward uplifting a people. Jesus fed the multitudes. The people of this contemporary era must understand, teach, and practice the principles of coexistence in this impersonal society.

"What use is it, my brethren, if a man says he has faith, but he has no works? Can that faith save him? If a brother or sister is without clothing and in need of daily food, and one of you says to them, 'Go in peace, be

warmed and be filled,' and yet you do not give
them what is necessary for their body, what
use is that? Even so faith, if it has no works,
is dead, being by itself." (James 2:14-17,
NASB)

Very real and practical needs must be met in building a nation. There has to be a commitment to eradicating hunger.

Covenant has to move from its sacred place as a church doctrine to practical living. *"And he would answer and say to them, 'Let the man who has two tunics share with him who has none; and let him who has food do likewise.'"* *(Luke 3:11, NASB)* The African American Christian Nation makes nourishing the poor a valid focus. Those who have the financial resources have to sow abundantly into the strengthening of others less fortunate.

> *"Instruct those who are rich in this present*
> *world not to be conceited or to fix their hope*
> *on the uncertainty of riches, but on God, who*
> *richly supplies us with all things to enjoy. In-*
> *struct them to do good, to be rich in good*
> *works, to be generous and ready to share."*
> (1 Timothy 6:17,18, NASB)

Food distribution is an essential start to building a nation geared to the physical, spiritual, and emotional needs of less fortunate individuals. An entire nation must be moved to this level of insight and covenant living.

Emergency food distribution centers will be placed throughout the communities to administer to the people's immediate necessities. Progress becomes highly visible when mere sustenance evolves into means to prohibit the return to the former state. Food co-ops will eventually become the more permanent fixture in the food program. Food co-ops will ensure that people get the most from limited budgets without sacrificing nutrition.

To remove the threat of stagnation, food production becomes a firm commitment. Land acquisitions will emerge for the raising of a food supply. Training will be provided in the cultivation and harvesting of food crops. This step will require the pooling of resources. Urbanites with economic stability must merge with those living in rural settings. This binding of urban and rural resources automatically knit the hearts of people together. Working together erases the estrangement caused by geography. People need people. People build a nation. People have to become aware and understand coexistence in this impersonal society.

"Moreover the profit of the earth is for all: the king himself is served by the field." (Ecclesiastes 5:9, KJV)

A stable food supply is of utmost importance for the African American Christian Nation.

8. DEPARTMENT OF CLOTHING

After emergency basic demands are met, a long-range program of manufacturing clothing has to be developed. Of course, the imagery attached to wearing certain name brands and styles must be combated. African American owned factories will be the settings for people to exercise a practical means of collective labor and faith. *"And all those who had believed were together, and had all things in common."* *(Acts 2:44, NASB)* People laboring together will produce community regeneration. This is a major endeavor to prohibit venders (from outside the African American ethnicity) and other influences from exploiting the needs of the people.

9. DEPARTMENT OF HOUSING

Housing needs are to be met as emergency requirements occur to swiftly move toward the eradication of homelessness from the African American Christian Nation. Organizing and pooling private resources will enable people without previous dreams of home ownership to do so. This will require training and developing all areas of resources.

"Enlarge the place of your tent; Stretch out the curtains of your dwellings, spare not;

Lengthen your cords, And strengthen your pegs. For you will spread abroad to the right and to the left. And your descendants will possess nations, And they will resettle the desolate cities." (Isaiah 54:2,3, NASB)

New life arises as areas of urban decay experience rebirth. Humility comes when the mercy of a nation is bestowed upon an individual. The African American Christian Nation will make full utilization of community land trusts.

10. DEPARTMENT OF EDUCATION

"The secret things belong to the Lord our God, but the things revealed belong to us and to our sons forever, that we may observe all the words of this law." (Deuteronomy 29:29, NASB)

The African American Christian Nation must develop schools with curricula designed for its own ethnicity as well as being Christian based. The education of the youth of the African American Christian Nation must be taken out of the hands of the public school system of indoctrination and antichrist orientation.

The social skills of young people cannot be left to a system which has already labeled them as failures. African American children, who place Jesus first and are properly trained academically, have an unlimited potential for success.

A greater definition of a support network for the children must be in place to afford them the third, fourth, or fifth chance to succeed in life. The educational system of the African American Christian Nation has to be a tool to develop ministry, culture, civic, economic, and academic empowerment. The covenant (promise) of God requires a constant reiteration that the young people will grasp living in covenant with God and community.

11. DEPARTMENT OF ECONOMIC BASE DEVELOPMENT

Economic bases are vitally needed. Sound economics will keep the youth returning and raising families in their communities. Through obedience to Jesus Christ and His teachings, the development of skills by the people can be turned into profitable earnings leading to a sound national economic base. Jesus can turn spiritually bankrupt people into an oasis of His power.

"Cast your bread on the surface of the waters, for you will find it after many days. Divide your portion to seven, or even to eight, for you do not know what misfortune may occur on the earth." (Ecclesiastes 11:1,2, NASB)

The economic stability of the African American Christian Nation will be in the diversity of its people. The limits on where African Americans can invest must be removed. The investment community has to become a global option. The resources and consumer power of African Americans has to become recognized as an available asset which will remain among African Americans.

12. DEPARTMENT OF PRISON MINISTRY

"The Spirit of the Lord God is upon me, Because the Lord has anointed me To bring good news to the afflicted; He has sent me to bind up the brokenhearted, To proclaim liberty to captives, And freedom to prisoners...." (Isaiah 61:1, NASB)

It is imperative that the vast power concentration of males and females confined in our prisons be returned to society as positive community resource persons. The Lord Jesus can reach behind prison bars and change the human heart.

"Thus says the Lord, 'In a favorable time I have answered You, And in a day of salvation I have helped You; And I will keep You and give You for a covenant of the people, To restore the land, to make them inherit the desolate heritages; Saying to those who are bound, 'Go forth,' To those who are in darkness, 'Show yourselves.' Along the roads they will feed, And their pasture will be on all bare heights." (Isaiah 49:8,9, NASB)

Vocational and specific skill training must be made available to those without marketable skills upon release from incarceration. Emotional and spiritual support has to be consistently and readily available to prevent the individual from returning to old habits and addictions.

This concentration of untapped and unrefined human resource need cultivation to reach productivity with the restoration of freedom. With the Holy Spirit as the guide, all men and women can lead productive lives.

CHAPTER 10

Exposing the
Slave Mentality

Exposing the Slave Mentality

Nothing retains dominance better than a slave-mentality. A slave-mentality may be defined as a human being owned as property and is absolutely subject to the will of another; a person who is completely dominated by some influence or divested of all freedom and personal rights. Mentality may be defined as the mental capacity, power of activity; the mental attitude or outlook: state of mind. We set forth a slave-mentality as the act of bringing another person under absolute subjection and ordering their mental attitude and activity. The slave-mentality is the acceptance of personal inferiority as the norm and thus accepting the domination by another.

A slave-mentality is not a myth, nor is it an excuse for a people's shortcomings. A slave-mentality is not an excuse for a victim to practice hatred toward an oppressor. In other words, a slave-mentality is not a justifiable reason for the opening of floodgates of hatred and prejudice. Although painful, the person bound by the slave-mentality cannot function without a slave-master to control his or her actions. This sensitive issue has been passed over for decades. Slave-mentality is an image created and reenforced to keep people in submission to a particular dominant force. Some religious systems (whether a single independent congregation or a denominational body) are often guilty of robbing its members of the freedom to make independent decisions. The control goes beyond spiritual oversight to total control of an individual or family. God gave men and women the freedom to make decisions. No matter how spiritual it may sound, no other man or woman has the right to exercise the removal or the deactivation of the decision-making process or mechanism from another human being.

Oppression is the same whether it derives from a religious system or a political system. Jesus charged His disciples, *"...Take heed, beware of the leaven of the Pharisees, and of the leaven of Herod." (Mark 8:15, KJV)* The end results of these two systems are the same when employed as tools of oppression. The people are spoiled of their potential and value by a slave-master figure. It is imperative that a clear statement is made here. No flesh is your enemy. However, Satan uses anyone he can. It does not matter to the devil if that individual is standing in the place of an angel of light.

The Scriptures bear witness that all people should exercise the God-given freedom to be a nation. Because of the Americanized slavery process, contemporary African Americans have not moved toward nationhood from a Christian prospective. This truth has been hidden by many African American religious leaders. Many of these African American religious leaders operate from their version of a slave-master mentality in order to suppress and retain control of their constituencies, who are bound by a slave mentality.

There is a definite need in the African American community to break the slave mentality. Unfortunately, a slave mentality is not easily broken. Many of the so-called shepherds of local Christian assemblies are slave masters rather than shepherds. These spiritual plantation owners use their position to stifle the freedom to think by the members of their congregation. The only thoughts arising from the people are those which originate from the minds of these church plantation taskmasters.

Under the disguise of church family, the total social involvement or noninvolvement of some churches are centered around activities which are exclusively designed by its leader. There would be nothing wrong with this association, if there were provision for independence and empowerment of individuals. The flock's political thoughts or non-thoughts are likewise dominated by these misinformed, non-informed, greedy, or totally naive leaders.

No political approach alone can bring reformation. Under the inspiration of the Holy Ghost, the Apostle Paul penned: *"Stand fast therefore in the liberty wherewith Christ hath made us free, and be not entangled again with the yoke of bondage." (Galatians 5:1, KJV)* The slave-master mentality and the slave mentality both must be annihilated. This calls for the dismissal of previous practices which are not based on truth.

Many so-called leaders are not warring for the liberation of a people, but rather personal inclusion in the existing system to gather a personal share of the spoils. In other words, the oppressed long to be like the oppressor. The hunger which drives the slave in such an instance is the slave's pulsation to be the master.

"No systematic effort toward change has been possible, for, taught the same economics, history, philosophy, literature and religion which have established the present code of morals, the Negro's mind has been brought under the control of his oppressor. The problem of holding the Negro down, therefore, is easily solved. When you control a man's thinking you do not have to worry about his actions. You do not have to tell him not to stand here or go yonder. He will find his 'proper place' and will stay in it. You do not need to send him to the back door. He will go without being told. In fact, if there is no back

door, he will cut one for his special benefit. His education makes it necessary. "[18]

Carter G. Woodson
The Mis-Education of the Negro

The devil has astutely transformed himself as an angel of light to destroy multitudes through religious bondage and oppression. Exploitation has become the desired end of controlling numbers of people. This factor is the governance practiced by so many religious leaders of color, and this is why this same segment of assumed leadership wars so hard against the truth regarding slave mentality and the slave-master mentality.

African Americans must have leadership that is bent on destroying the slave mentality and resisting the temptation to employ the slave-master mentality!

The African American Christian Nation is the truth which will expose man-made religious kingdoms no matter how petty or large. The freedom that God desires for African Americans is to walk by faith into nationhood! The despised of the earth are the people of God who will confound the wise. It is those African Americans (debtors, victims, distressed, discontented, and hungry for the power and empowerment of God) who will emerge to lead this movement to nationhood. It is this group who will

---

[18]Woodson, Carter Godwin. *The Mis-Education of the Negro.* AMS Press, Inc., Revised 1977, pg. xiii.

emerge from the cave experience of the infancy of this movement to leadership that will redefine the direction of a people.

CHAPTER
11

Heritage and
Culture

Heritage and Culture

"OUT OF THE DUST OF AFRICA...

"IN THE MYTHOPOEIC WORLD of the ear-
liest biblical authors, it was believed that in
the beginning man was formed 'from the dust
of the earth.' This very 'dust' was envisioned
as the soil of Africa. Accordingly, generic
man was African/Edenic; generic man in a
word was black by modern classifications of
racial typologies. Whether you interpret Adam
to have been an individual or a nation of
people, it is clear that there was one Father
(God) and one mother (earth). The earth was
of African/Edenic. From this point, we con-
tinue our study of the biblical records in the
sure knowledge that if the root of the family
tree of man was African/Edenic, then all sub-
sequent branches of that tree must give ac-
knowledgment and respect to the source from
which they came...the facts will point out in

111

this context that the reference to people as being either Hamitic or Semitic does not denote racially different peoples, but rather people of a common racial heritage who developed different cultural life-styles."[19]

The Original African Heritage Study Bible
Introduction

The African American Christian Nation must refuse to allow others to define its heritage and culture apart from what God has already promised. It is inclusive and not exclusive. *"For we can do nothing against the truth, but only for the truth." (2 Corinthians 13:8, NASB)* Jesus remains the door of entrance. As we enter into heavenly citizenship, African Americans do not have to forfeit their heritage and culture. Jesus never renounced His Jewish heritage and culture. Jesus desires that we walk in all His example.

The African American Christian Nation is a work exemplifying the demand which Jesus placed on the rich young ruler. In order to gain this new station, you have to sell the old to gain the new treasure. Those who are able to respond as Jesus calls will discover the hundredfold blessing, a blessing which far exceeds that which is currently being grasped. *"But many who are first, will be last; and the last, first." (Mark 10:31, NASB)*

---

[19]Felder, Cain Hope. *The Original African Heritage Study Bible.* Nashville: The James C. Winston Publishing Company, 1993, pg. xiii.

African Americans were stripped of their heritage and culture through the Americanized slavery process. The decision to become a nation is the only course for this thirty-million-plus people to gain respect and dignity.

Cultural loyalty is a step of boldness. There are a great number of African Americans who have totally bought into the Eurocentric culture and have no desire to be a part of launching the African American Christian Nation. They feel that too much is being made of this "African stuff." They are to be pitied. They have made a conscious choice to be identified with the Eurocentric culture. In the sense of the spirit realm, it was equally a tough fight for some people to give up the sinful culture and take on the righteous culture of Jesus Christ. In making such a choice, an individual renounces their heritage. It is much like Esau selling his heritage or birthright for a bowl of soup. **Many African Americans sell their inheritance or heritage for a small bowl of acceptance in a society never designed for them.** Those founding fathers of this nation wrote documents which never included men and women of African descent as being fully human; therefore, the design of their nation was never to include African Americans.

Understanding the difficulty of some people to give up a party for holiness, it is easy to understand their unwillingness to leave the party given by someone else to take on the responsibility of calling a people to righteousness. To abandon the culture of a nation with which an individual is familiar to pioneer something totally new, this presents a cause for alarm. It is alarming to the one who has relied on someone else to define his or her heritage and culture. When you have learned to rely on the borrowed, it is very difficult to peer into the unknown and see self-reliance. Self-reliance is blurred all the more when the sure pain of separation from the borrowed is quite visible. At such intervals, the knowledge of what God states as one's heritage and culture makes the steps sure. *"Thy word is a lamp to my feet, And a light to my path." (Psalm 119:105, NASB)*

CHAPTER
12

Vision of
Deliverance

Vision of Deliverance

THE CHILDREN OF GOD need to join their hearts for peace and compassion toward all mankind. One segment of humanity cannot be left out. God's higher call for African Americans is nationhood.

> *"Who has heard such a thing? Who has seen such things? Can a land be born in one day? Can a nation be brought forth all at once? As soon as Zion travailed, she also brought forth her sons."* (Isaiah 66:8, NASB)
>
> *"But God has chosen the foolish things of the world to shame the wise, and God has chosen the weak things of the world to shame the things which are strong, and the base things of the world and the despised, God has chosen, the things that are not, that He might nullify the things that are."* (1 Corinthians 1:27,28, NASB)

Nothing is too hard for the Lord. He is still calling forth a people to walk by faith and believe His Word! A nation is but a drop in the bucket to the Lord. It is not a monumental task for Him to raise up a nation. He is the eternal God. He speaks and whatever He desires He performs!

Those of the African Diaspora in the United States must assume their rightful position in Christ and be the nation which He is calling them to be.

Abram's family and friends probably thought him foolish for starting out on a journey not knowing his destination. He obeyed God and became the friend of the Almighty!

As a nation (The African American Christian Nation), African Americans will proceed to renounce the works of the devil which has labeled them as failures and co-dependents on the handouts of others. The African American Christian Nation summons and challenges people of all nations to respect the dignity assigned her by God Almighty! This respect must begin within African Americans themselves.

Bringing together two opposite peoples (people who hate themselves and people who do love themselves) to form a nation is a work of the Holy Spirit. No amount of human ingenuity could possibly accomplish such a feat. The African American Christian Nation is the perfect vehicle for such a difficult challenge. To arrive at nationhood, everything that can be shaken will be shaken. A great number of personal kingdoms must fall. God anointed David to be king while Saul was still on the throne. God's timing baffles and defies the plans and outlooks of men. God remains sovereign!

The challenge (which is no challenge to God at all) is helping people of African descent realize their potential by living covenant and exercising divine principles attached with being an existing nation. The work ahead looms difficult, but not insurmountable. So many African Americans (influential and non-influential) look for salvation in assimilation of European culture and spiritual directives. It is difficult for these leaders and their followers to address or adhere to nationhood as a responsible issue, because they have to break first from a slave-mentality; a state which is very painful to acknowledge as being part of one's makeup. Prayer, travailing intercessory prayer, will bring forth the African American Christian Nation. *"...as soon as Zion travailed, she also brought forth her sons." (Isaiah 66:8, NASB)*

The spiritual law, the natural law, and the reality of the matter acknowledge that African Americans are indeed a new people (not fully African and certainly not fully American). Because African Americans have not raised their people to the consciousness of being a nation, other nations do not take this great body of people seriously. Freedom from slavery did not render true freedom, because African Americans were not given nationhood status. As a result, every plague to come upon this vast continent of North America has found fertile growth in the congregation of African Americans. *The African American Christian Nation is an evangelistic tool to bring together a people stricken by poverty, illiteracy, cultural deprivement, and spiritual disarray!*

Love is the way to propel this revolution. African Americans face the task of loving themselves into nationhood! Faith works by love! The task of showing, displaying, and giving love through social action and justice is not an impossible feat for people moving into nationhood. Unity, monitored by constant communion with the Heavenly Father, is the only requirement for individuals moving toward nationhood.

The African American Christian Nation is not a foreign concept to God. It is only strange in the ears of those who *choose* to speak a different language. It is strange only to those who do not have an ear to hear what the Spirit has to say.

Summary

"If there is no struggle, there is no progress. Those who profess to favor freedom and yet depreciate agitation, are men who want crops without plowing up the ground, they want rain without thunder and lightning. They want the ocean without the awful roar of its many waters. *Power concedes nothing without a demand. It never did and it never will.*"[20]

Frederick Douglas
Abolitionist

"Above all, we must be reminded anew that God is at work in His universe. He is not outside the world looking on with a sort of cold indifference. Here on all the roads of life, He is striving in our striving. Like an ever-loving Father, He is working through history for the salvation of His chil-

---

[20]An excerpt from a speech given by Frederick Douglas, abolitionist.

dren. As we struggle to defeat the forces of evil, the God of the universe struggles with us. Evil dies on the seashore, not merely because of man's endless struggle against it, but because of God's power to defeat it."[21]

Rev. Dr. Martin Luther King Jr.
Strength to Love

"It was during those long and lonely years that my hunger for the freedom of my own people became a hunger for the freedom of all people, white and black. I knew as well as I knew anything that the oppressor must be liberated just as surely as the oppressed. A man who takes away another man's freedom is a prisoner of hatred, he is locked behind the bars of prejudice and narrow-mindedness. I am not truly free if I am taking away someone else's freedom, just as surely as I am not free when my freedom is taken from me. The oppressed and the oppressor alike are robbed of their humanity.

"When I walked out of prison, that was my mission, to liberate the oppressed and the oppressor both."[22]

Nelson Mandela
Long Walk to Freedom

---

[21]King, Jr. Martin Luther. *Strength to Love*. Philadelphia: Fortress Press, 1981, pg. 83.
[22]Mandela, Nelson Rolihlahla. *Long Walk to Freedom*. Boston: Little, Brown and Company, 1994, pg. 544.

THE PERSON COMMITTED to understand or desirous to understand the movement toward the African American Christian Nation will discover statements from each chapter which may be used for enlightening discussion and a trigger for further biblical, historical, and social study.

The highlights are verbatim quotes. Each quotation is intended to be a thought-provoking mechanism on the subject of the African American Christian Nation and an extraction of sincere prayer for the same.

SECTION ONE
Why the Struggle to Be a Nation?

Chapter One
An African American Christian Nation

◆ African Americans, living on the soil of these United States of America, are the only people on the face of the earth who are not recognized as a nation nor belonging to a nation.

◆ There are distinct blessings from God which are bestowed upon a people when they recognize themselves as a nation.

◆ The African American Christian Nation may never be embraced by all African Americans; however, that would not minimize its validity.

◆ African Americans must remove from their thought patterns the imagery of conquering or possessing the land of others before nationhood can be appreciated.

◆ Above all, if you cannot see or commit to the vision, do not allow the devil to use you as a snare or one who blinds others!

Chapter Two
From Oppression to Nationhood

◆ This nation (United States of America) was never designed to include African Americans in ways other than a cheap labor pool or sordid pleasure to morbid minds.

◆ The Catholics have acted on the divine principle of nationhood. The pope operates from his headquarters in the Vatican, an autonomous nation. African Americans must begin asking the question, why not the African American Christian Nation?

◆ The African American Christian Nation must be declared unashamedly and without inhibitions!

Chapter Three
Declaration of Nationhood

◆ Every people have the God mandate to be free and to be a nation!

◆ It is God's design for people to arise to nation-hood status and have one of their own to rule over them.

◆ When someone rules over you, who is not your brother or sister or a member of your own na-tion, that nation is in disobedience to God! In nationhood, African Americans will have the opportunity to show, produce and develop among themselves loyalty, discipline, commitment, community, strength, and worship.

Chapter Four
Declaration of Freedom

◆ Freedom brings harmonious living and the prac-tice of justice.

◆ No political system, racist society, nor economic caste system can deny freedom to the nation sub-mitted to God; neither can be denied that which cries from the depth of man, for freedom is in his spirit.

SECTION TWO
What Is the Pillar for the Nation?

Chapter Five
Truth as a Foundation

◆ Truth is the only liberating factor! That which will eliminate false hope and provide a secure future must be proclaimed.

◆ When the proper perspective of who one really is, is fully realized, the issue of being part of a nation ceases to be a question. It only stands to reason that poor self-esteem would be advocated by forces which do not desire a people to emerge into a nation.

◆ The arrest of callous individualism will allow nationalism to take root in the growth of young minds. Corporate gains will be sought rather than individual accolades.

◆ Personal acceptance must relinquish its grip to a people focused on the purpose and intent of a nation's birth.

◆ The masterful maintenance of other systems by the intellect and knowledge of African Americans is more than credible to start up and maintain a nation. It is a biblical principle that you should not obtain your own until you have proven faithful over that which belongs to another.

Chapter Six
Economic Focus

◆ African Americans must recognize and understand clearly the struggle for economic, cultural, spiritual, and national identity.

◆ The African American Christian Nation sends a message that African Americans can no longer be viewed as consumers only. The people of the African American community deserve an opportunity to become producers in their own community.

Chapter Seven
Commitment to Unity and Service

◆ It is imperative to state that brethren cannot have true unity without nationhood. To exist as a non-nation, African Americans cut themselves off from this very potential. Without a nation, it is every man to his own tent.

◆ The African American Christian Nation is not an escape artist tactic to evade servanthood. In fact, it is the beckoning to the higher call of servanthood: commitment.

Chapter Eight
Legitimate Governing Apparatus

◆ No government can operate without a foundational promise which assures the people of equality and justice.

◆ Before there can be a congress or parliament, there must be a foundation of righteousness and holiness. Justice must flow from the Spirit of God.

◆ A commitment to justice is a commitment to God and the people.

◆ Anything less than African Americans becoming a nation will not accomplish the work God has assigned to this people.

SECTION THREE
How to Enact the Nation

Chapter Nine
Departments of the Cabinet

◆ The light has come to illuminate the path leading from chaos and destruction to peace and prosperity.

Chapter Ten
Exposing the Slave Mentality

◆ The Scriptures bear witness that all people should exercise the God-given freedom to be a nation. Because of the Americanized slavery process, contemporary African Americans have not moved toward nationhood from a Christian prospective.

◆ Oppression is the same whether it derives from a religious system or a political system.

Chapter Eleven
Heritage and Culture

◆ The African American Christian Nation must refuse to allow others to define its heritage and culture apart from what God has already promised. It is inclusive and not exclusive.

◆ **Many African Americans sell their inheritance or heritage for a small bowl of acceptance in a society never designed for them.**

◆ When you have learned to rely on the borrowed, it is very difficult to peer into the unknown and see self-reliance. Self-reliance is blurred all the more when the sure pain of separation from the borrowed is quite visible.

Chapter Twelve
Vision of Deliverance

◆ As a nation (The African American Christian Nation), African Americans will proceed to renounce the works of the devil which has labeled them as failures and co-dependents on the hand-outs of others. The African American Christian Nation summons and challenges people of all nations to respect the dignity assigned her by God Almighty!

◆ The spiritual law, the natural law, and the reality of the matter acknowledge that African Americans are indeed a new people (not fully African and certainly not fully American). Because African Americans have not raised their people to the consciousness of being a nation, other nations do not take this great body of people seriously.

◆ The African American Christian Nation is an evangelistic tool to bring together a people stricken by poverty, illiteracy, cultural deprivement, and spiritual disarray!

◆ The African American Christian Nation is not a foreign concept to God, it is only strange in the ears of those who *choose* to speak a different language. It is strange only to those who do not have an ear to hear what the Spirit has to say.

The African American Christian Nation

PHASE I: This biblical truth must be gotten out to the multitudes. It must not only come from the pulpits, but it must ring from the hearts of believers everywhere. It must become a witnessing tool to bring people into the family of God. It must become an individual's responsibility to tell his or her neighbor.

PHASE II: This work marks the beginning. This is your opportunity to be a part of divine history! Will you take the first step by forming a local chapter of the African American Christian Nation in your area? Call (216) 752-7727 today!

PURPOSE: There is an urgency to save our young people and ensure them all the blessings of God for the future! This is our chance to leave a legacy to a generation twisted by the imageries of darkness!

About the Author

The Reverend Mark C. Olds holds the unique distinction (dual firsts) of receiving the rites of ministry ordination and pastoring a church inside a penal colony. These two feats were accomplished while Mark C. Olds was serving an active sentence of 55 years in the Federal Bureau of Prison System.

Rev. Dr. Harold A. Carter, Sr., pastor of New Shiloh Baptist Church, served as moderator of the presbytery of the Baptist Ministers Conference of Baltimore and Vicinity — conducting this very sacred occasion inside the federal prison at Lewisburg, Pennsylvania, on December 1, 1984. This action forever remains a part of divine history.

Another witness of divine favor upon Mark C. Olds' life was manifested in his release from prison after serving ten consecutive years without having to meet a parole board. The consistency of his walk of faith preceded him.

Rev. Mark C. Olds performs multiple labors for the advancement of the kingdom of God and the enhancement of African American people. In July of 1994, he founded the Covenant Gathering Christian Church (Church of God). In April of 1995, he took on an additional role as assistant to the pastor, Rev. Dr. Otis Moss, Jr., at the Olivet Institutional Baptist Church, Cleveland, Ohio. "Laboring with a new ministry while gaining experience from an established ministry enhances my serving the people of the African American community in the vast promises of God." He is also the founder and Executive Director of Community Resource Inc., Cleveland, Ohio. Mark C. Olds is a Master's candidate in the Master's Nonprofit Organization Program at Case Western Reserve University, Cleveland, Ohio.

The African American Christian Nation Needs You!

Send your resume immediately to:
> **The African American Christian Nation**
> **Attention: Reverend Mark C. Olds**
> **3550 Warrensville Center Road**
> **Suite 101 South**
> **Shaker Heights, Ohio 44122**

For more information on the African American Christian Nation or to speak personally with Reverend Mark C. Olds, you may call 1-216-752-7727.

Please act today. A nation is waiting to be birthed!